TUCSON TREASURES

RECIPES & REFLECTIONS

Tucson Medical Center Auxiliary

This cookbook is a collection of favorite recipes,
which are not necessarily original recipes.

TUCSON TREASURES
RECIPES & REFLECTIONS

Published by
Tucson Medical Center Auxiliary

Copyright © 1999 by
Tucson Medical Center Auxiliary
5301 East Grant Road
Tucson, Arizona 85733
520-324-5355

Library of Congress Number: 99-071086
ISBN: 0-9670247-0-6

Edited, designed, and manufactured by
Favorite Recipes® Press
an imprint of

FRP

P.O. Box 305142
Nashville, Tennessee 37230
1-800-358-0560

Book Design: Steve Newman
Project Manager: Charlene Sproles
Project Coordinator: Carolyn King

Manufactured in the United States of America
First Printing: 1999   10,000 copies

Dedication

We wish to thank the family and friends of Elsie Taylor for contributions made to the Tucson Medical Center Auxiliary in her memory. Elsie was a longtime Auxilian who had a special interest in photography, and who photographed many auxiliary events over a number of years. These contributed funds have been used to defray the cost of the photographs in *Tucson Treasures*. The photographs in this book are dedicated to Elsie Taylor.

Cameron Sandhowe was a member of the *Tucson Treasures* Committee, and an Auxilian for many years. Cameron passed away before our book went to press. The recipes in this book are dedicated to Cameron Sandhowe.

Acknowledgments

The photographs in this book are the work of Edna Foster, a Tucson Medical Center Auxilian, and Eileen Schwab, Tucson Medical Center photographer. The line art was prepared by William Foster, a Tucson Medical Center Auxilian. The Committee is grateful to these three individuals for their artistic talents.

Preface

The Tucson area has many "treasures": the city of Tucson, a true treasure; the Tucson Medical Center, a true community treasure; and the Tucson Medical Center Auxiliary, a most treasured organization. In celebration of fifty years of volunteer service that Auxilians have given to the patients, families, and staff of the Tucson Medical Center, the Auxiliary is publishing this cookbook.

In *Tucson Treasures* we celebrate our fifty years with many great recipes collected by the Auxiliary. We also celebrate a wealth of outstanding and unique things that make the Tucson area special. You will find both photographs and information regarding many of these wonderful "treasures."

To Our Volunteers—A Love Poem

Our patients come first, and TMC stands
for healing and caring from capable hands.
The tasks are so many, the hours so few,
yet all of it works because we have you.
Dedication and humor, a tear and a laugh,
you're comforting patients or helping the staff.
Our babies have bonnets with stitches that hide
a lacy white hanky for some blushing bride.
Directions to steer someone down the right hall;
if they don't speak English, no problem at all!
Our own sparkling shop full of laughter and fun,
with just the right gifts to please everyone.
We have papers and orders and forms neatly filed;
and a soft, gentle touch—soothing a child.
We don't have elves, we have craft ladies instead—
skilled hands making magic from fabric and thread.
The Patient Assistants walk mile after mile,
and flowers arrive attached to a smile.

Too tired for the walk? No reason to worry.
Rest for a bit, while strong hands guide the surrey.
That event of the year, our holiday star—
BEST SALE IN TOWN—the Christmas Bazaar.
The Surgery lobby might be a sad place
except for kind words and a bright smiling face.
Your hands and your smiles, the voices that lift;
your giving of time—that most precious gift.
So many reasons for thanks and for cheers
on this special day for our own volunteers.
In our scheme of things, you each have a part.
Whatever you do, you are TMC's heart!

Mary Hungate, Director of Printing Services for many years, now retired, wrote this poem to honor Tucson Medical Center Auxilians, to whom she was a wonderful friend and tireless supporter.

Contents

Tucson Treasures Committee

Marjorie Bailie
Doral Baird
Lou Bankson
Martha Bortle
Sue Christie
Arlene Crawford
Kitty Davis
Mary De Acetis
Norma Fletcher
Edna Foster
William Foster
Cathy Glazebrook
Shirley Gould

Gail Greeley
Jeanne Grove
Marjorie Heath
Helen Ivory
Patricia Knoblock
Barbara Lawrie
David Lilley
Barbara Marks
Carolyn Matson
Janet Milliron
Nancy Nelson
Nicey Randall
Beverly Reed
Tom Rees

Pat Reinhart
Helen Reynolds
Marian Rogerson
Cameron Sandhowe
Gloria Scaletta
Margaret Schmidt
Eileen Schwab
Glenna Smith
Harriet Spiesman
Mildred Spillane
Marian Tapas
Jerie Vaughn
Celia Wood

To Our Volunteers

Valuable volunteers like you make us beam,
Outstanding in the comfort you bring to our team,
Loyal and supportive in your heartfelt way,
Untiring in the efforts you offer each day,
Notable for the warmth of your special touch,
Tender yet strong when it means so very much,
Eager to share both your hope and a smile,
Encouraging all as a part of your style,
Rating our highest appreciation for all that you do,
Special and precious!
That's what we call volunteers like you!

Tucson

Early Tucson villagers, it has been discovered, farmed corn, used tobacco, and shot one another in the back using arrowheads, but this was 760 B.C. They occupied sites along the Santa Cruz River, which had water most of the year. A settlement designated Santa Cruz Bend contained 176 pit dwellings, storehouses, and communal structures. The occupants foraged for food, grew corn with the aid of irrigation ditches, and buried their dead in the earliest-known formal cemetery in southern Arizona. These Late Archaic people were followed by the Mogollon, Anasazi, and Hohokam tribes. The first two were nomadic but the Hohokam were farmers and traders who mysteriously disappeared in the late 1400s.

Spanish explorers arrived in the 1500s to find a settlement occupied by Pima Indians. Located at the base of a black volcanic rock mountain, the village was called Stjukshon (variously spelled). Father Eusebio Francisco Kino stopped at the village in 1698 and returned several years later to build missions in the area, the most notable being San Xavier del Bac south of present-day Tucson. However, Spanish influence was feeble at this time and Apache raiders were beginning to move west into the Tucson basin. In 1775, the Spanish laid out the Presidio of San Augustin del Tucson. Apache raids made fortification necessary, so walls twelve feet high surrounded the fledgling community.

Mexico inherited Tucson from the Spanish after a revolution in 1821, but little changed except the flag. In 1854, Tucson joined the United States with the Gadsden Purchase but it was two years before protection in the form of the Army's First Dragoons arrived. Adventurous Americans began to head west to Tucson despite Apache assaults, and soon the Butterfield Overland Stage opened service to the area. The 1860s were Tucson's Wild West years and most men were armed. Shoot-outs were frequent, but the town prospered and served as territorial capital from 1867 to 1877. The railroad came to town in 1880 and brought a new growth spurt, further fueled by the establishment of the University of Arizona in 1891.

Tucson today is a vibrant city that continues to grow at a rapid rate. Mild winters, a dry climate, the mountains, and the friendly population attract thousands of new residents every year. Long a popular retirement area, Tucson has a reputation for high tech industry that is bringing in a younger, well educated populace who seem to thrive on the Hispanic influence on culture and architecture.

Tucson Medical Center Auxiliary

From its inception in 1943, Tucson Medical Center never lacked for volunteers from the community. At its October 1945 meeting, the Board of Directors asked Margaret Knight to chair an auxiliary committee. By February 1946, ten women, known as Medical Center Volunteers, were supplementing the activities of the hospital staff. At the January 1947 Board of Directors meeting, Miss Knight was asked to explore the possibility of organizing a TMC woman's auxiliary. Miss Knight dutifully organized a meeting with ladies from the community but since most of them already belonged to groups performing volunteer duties at TMC, a plan was not implemented.

In 1948, a Citizen's Advisory Board composed of 100 members was formed to help inform the community about the hospital and to aid in fund-raising. Miss Knight loudly protested that the newly formed board was made up entirely of men. So she was authorized to form a similar board composed entirely of women. The fifteen women attending the first meeting formed the nucleus of today's auxiliary. This core group immediately pledged to recruit new members and provided volunteer coverage of the reception desk and the book cart, and formed a volunteer motor corps.

The volunteers started wearing uniforms in early 1949 and thus were distinguished from the other volunteers serving the hospital. The Tucson Medical Center Auxiliary was officially established in November of 1949 with fifty members and a very small treasury.

As with any organization, there have been many, many changes over the past fifty years. Auxilians are found in every part of the hospital. Fund-raising efforts never cease, but the methods reflect the changing times. New uniforms evoke lots of comments. What doesn't change is the unflagging devotion of the men, women, and young people, members of the TMC Auxiliary, who willingly give their time and their talents to a very important community asset.

Appetizers & Relishes

Deviled Ham Puffs

24 slices bread
8 ounces cream cheese, softened
1 egg yolk
1 teaspoon onion juice or grated onion
1/2 teaspoon baking powder
Salt to taste
2 (4-ounce) cans deviled ham

Cut one 2½-inch round from each bread slice. Place the bread rounds in a single layer on a baking sheet. Broil until toasted on 1 side; set aside.

Combine the cream cheese, egg yolk, onion juice, baking powder and salt in a bowl. Spread the ham on the untoasted sides of the bread rounds. Spoon a mound of the cheese mixture over the ham on each round.

Bake at 375 degrees for 10 to 12 minutes or until puffed and golden brown.

Makes Twenty-Four Appetizers

Rye Bites

1 pound ground beef
1 pound bulk hot pork sausage
1 teaspoon oregano
$1/2$ teaspoon pepper
1 pound Velveeta cheese, cubed
50 slices party rye bread

Brown the ground beef and pork sausage in a skillet, stirring until crumbly; drain well. Stir in the oregano and pepper. Add the cheese, stirring until completely melted.

Spread the ground beef mixture on the rye bread slices. Place on baking sheets. Broil until bubbly.

Note: May place assembled appetizers on baking sheets and freeze before broiling. Remove from the baking sheets and store in sealed plastic bags until ready to use.

Makes Fifty Appetizers

Why Volunteer?

The reasons for volunteering at Tucson Medical Center are as varied as the individuals involved. One gentleman freely admitted he wanted to find a wife. He didn't and moved on. Fortunately, most people have slightly more altruistic motives. Many of our volunteers are retired and find they have extra time on their hands. Others have had a positive experience with the hospital and wish to give something in return. Still others work full time but manage to schedule a volunteer experience once a week. Whatever the reason, they are a welcome addition to the hospital staff. They bring enthusiasm and a wealth of experience to their volunteer jobs and are encouraged to participate in the administration of the Auxiliary. Why volunteer? Altruism is important. Personal satisfaction is important. Being part of the TMC family is important. As stated earlier, the reasons are varied. The most important thing is the act of volunteering.

Cocktail Meatballs

2 pounds ground beef
1 cup bread crumbs
1 envelope onion soup mix
3 eggs
1 (16-ounce) can sauerkraut, drained
1 (16-ounce) can whole berry cranberry
*   sauce*
1 (12-ounce) bottle chili sauce
1½ cups water
1 cup packed brown sugar

Combine the ground beef, bread crumbs, onion soup mix and eggs in a bowl and mix well. Shape into 1-inch meatballs. Place the meatballs in a 3-quart baking dish.

Combine the sauerkraut, cranberry sauce, chili sauce, water and brown sugar in a bowl and mix well. Spoon over the meatballs.

Bake, covered, at 350 degrees for 1½ hours, stirring occasionally. Uncover the baking dish. Bake for 30 minutes longer or until the meatballs are cooked through.

Serve Eight

ARIZONA
BUILDING

Slow-Roasted Tomatoes

30 plum tomatoes
2 tablespoons olive oil
1 teaspoon sugar
$^1/_2$ teaspoon salt
Freshly ground pepper

Cut the tomatoes lengthwise into halves. Place in a bowl. Add 1$^1/_2$ tablespoons of the oil, tossing to coat. Arrange the tomato halves cut side up on a large baking sheet. Sprinkle with the sugar, salt and pepper.

Roast at 325 degrees for 2$^1/_2$ to 3 hours or until the tomatoes start to brown and are almost dry. (They should look like dried apricots and hold their shape.) Cool to room temperature. Brush with the remaining $^1/_2$ tablespoon oil before serving.

Note: May freeze in plastic containers or store in a jar with olive oil to cover and refrigerate for up to 10 days.

Serves Eight to Ten

Patient Assistance

"Hello, Mrs. Brown. My name is Suzie and I'm a volunteer with the TMC Auxiliary Patient Assistance program. Is everything all right in your room? Does your TV work properly? Is the temperature in the room okay? Would you like an extra blanket? How about a magazine?"

All newly admitted patients are visited by a Patient Assistance volunteer to ascertain if there are any unanticipated problems. These can often be solved by the volunteer with a phone call or a conversation with unit personnel. A card with the phone number of the Auxiliary office is left with each patient should concerns arise or if the patient desires another visit.

The volunteer leaves the room usually hearing "Thanks a lot for stopping by."

Spanish Assistance

Tucson Medical Center is truly a bilingual facility. With Tucson located so near Mexico, many patients and visitors bring an Hispanic influence in both culture and language to the hospital. The need for translators became apparent very early on. It was essential to have people who could translate doctors' orders, assist clergy and other personnel, and assist individuals in finding their way around a large complex. In 1976, the Spanish Assistance

Service was formed by Tucson Medical Center Auxiliary. These Auxilians are available in person or by phone to provide translation. In addition, the Education Department offers Spanish classes to employees. Patient Assistance Auxilians leave pamphlets printed in Spanish and English with all new patients. Signs throughout the hospital are printed in both languages.

The people who offer help to the lost and frustrated at a time of stress and worry truly seem to wear halos and wings.

ARIZONA BUILDING

Cheesy Spinach Quiche

1/2 cup melted margarine or butter
1/2 cup egg substitute or 2 eggs
1 cup milk
1/2 (10-ounce) package frozen chopped
   spinach, thawed
1/3 cup finely chopped onion
2 1/4 cups shredded Cheddar cheese
1 cup flour
1 teaspoon baking powder
1 teaspoon salt

Combine the melted margarine, egg
substitute and milk in a large bowl. Drain the
spinach, squeezing any remaining liquid
from the spinach. Stir the spinach, onion and
cheese into the milk mixture.

Combine the flour, baking powder and
salt in a bowl. Add to the milk mixture,
stirring well. Pour into a greased 9x13-inch
baking dish.

Bake at 350 degrees for 30 to 35 minutes
or until the quiche just begins to brown.
Cool and cut into 20 squares.

Note: May be prepared in advance and
frozen. To reheat, bake at 350 degrees for
about 20 minutes.

Serves Twenty

Hot Cheesy Artichoke Dip

2 (6-ounce) jars oil-marinated artichoke
   hearts
8 ounces cream cheese, softened
3/4 cup grated Parmesan cheese
1/2 cup sour cream
1/2 cup mayonnaise
Pepper to taste

Drain the artichokes, reserving a small
amount of the marinade. Chop the artichokes
into small pieces.

Combine the artichokes, reserved
marinade, cream cheese, Parmesan cheese,
sour cream, mayonnaise and pepper in a
bowl and mix well. Spoon into a 9x13-inch
baking dish, spreading evenly.

Bake at 350 degrees for 30 minutes or
until hot and bubbly. Serve with crackers.

Makes About Three Cups

The Arizona Building

The Arizona Building, a two-story adobe structure, was built in 1927 as a nurses' residence for Desert Sanatorium staff. Four nurses—two from Canada, one from Scotland, and one from New York City—resided there. These ladies, accustomed to large metropolitan hospitals, took one look at the desert area with a few adobe buildings far from civilization—and an abundance of cacti, snakes, and scorpions—and were ready to get on the next train out of town.

They stayed, however. In 1928, a pool was built that provided relaxation and cooling during the long hot summers. These stalwart ladies paid ten dollars a month for room and board and earned the magnificent sum of $125.00 monthly. A bus ran twice a day into the "city," but during World War II a serious housing shortage meant that eighty employees lived on the Desert Sanatorium campus, many of them in a very crowded nurses' quarters. In 1946, a cooler was installed, paid for in part by the nurses. Over the years, with roads and transportation improving, the nurses moved out and an assortment of students occupied the building while

studying at what was now Tucson Medical Center. In 1975, the building was remodeled to accommodate the National Foundation of Allergy and Asthma Clinic.

In 1981, the Tucson Medical Center Auxiliary moved into the first floor of the building, with the second floor housing a variety of TMC offices. The Auxiliary utilizes every inch of space with meeting rooms, offices, a kitchen, and storage areas. The old building looks lovely when decorated for parties, teas, Christmas festivities, and other programs. This special building has such a fascinating history. How amazed those first nurses would be to learn what their residence has gone through these past seventy years.

Easy Dilly Dip

1 cup sour cream
1 cup mayonnaise
1½ teaspoons Beau Monde seasoning
1 teaspoon parsley flakes, crushed
1 teaspoon dillweed
1 teaspoon minced onion

Combine the sour cream, mayonnaise, Beau Monde seasoning, parsley flakes, dillweed and onion in a bowl, blending well. Refrigerate, covered, for 1 hour. Serve with cut-up carrots, celery, broccoli and chips for dipping or as a topping for baked potatoes.

Makes Two Cups

Egg Chive Dip

8 ounces chive-flavor soft cream cheese
¼ cup mayonnaise
½ teaspoon salt
¼ teaspoon pepper
¼ teaspoon Worcestershire sauce
4 hard-cooked eggs, finely chopped

Beat the cream cheese in a bowl until fluffy. Stir in the mayonnaise, salt, pepper and Worcestershire sauce. Add the hard-cooked eggs and blend well. Refrigerate, covered, for 1 hour. Serve with assorted cut-up vegetables and crackers.

Serves Eight

Quick-and-Easy Spanish Dip

1 pound ground beef
1 sweet onion, chopped
1 (16-ounce) jar thick and chunky salsa
1 (15-ounce) jar medium-hot picante
*   con queso dip*

Brown the ground beef with the onion in a
large skillet; drain. Add the salsa and cheese
dip. Cook until heated through, stirring
occasionally. Serve with tortilla chips.

Note: May be prepared a day in advance,
refrigerated, covered, and reheated
before serving.

Makes About Six Cups

Traveling Taco Dip

1 (16-ounce) can refried beans
2 cups sour cream
8 ounces frozen guacamole, thawed
1 (7-ounce) can diced green chiles,
*   drained*
1 (7-ounce) can black olives, drained
*   and diced*
2 plum tomatoes, diced
4 ounces shredded Cheddar cheese

Spread the refried beans over the bottom of
a 10-inch pie plate. Top with layers of sour
cream, guacamole, green chiles, black olives,
tomatoes and cheese. Refrigerate, covered,
until chilled. Serve with tortilla chips.

Serves Eight to Ten

18

Celebrity Pineapple Cheese Ball

16 ounces cream cheese, softened
1 (8-ounce) can crushed pineapple,
   drained
2 cups chopped pecans
$1/4$ cup finely chopped green bell pepper
2 teaspoons finely chopped onion
1 teaspoon seasoned salt

Beat the cream cheese in a medium
bowl until smooth. Stir in the pineapple,
1 cup of the pecans, green pepper, onion
and seasoned salt gradually.

Shape the cheese mixture into a ball.
Roll in the remaining 1 cup pecans. Wrap
in plastic wrap or foil. Refrigerate for 8 to
10 hours.

Place the cheese ball on a large serving
board or plate and surround with crackers.
Garnish with pineapple slices, maraschino
cherries or parsley.

Serves Forty

Heart Pillows

*The Sewing Group of Tucson
Medical Center Auxiliary makes
heart-shaped pillows in colorful
fabrics to be given to those patients
undergoing cardiac surgery. The
patient hugs the pillow to the chest
when coughing, and the very firm
pillow acts as a splint to ease the
pain. Patients returning to the
hospital for further surgery often
bring their "life saver" pillow with
them, a poignant affirmation of a
great idea.*

Mock Liver Pâté

1 medium onion, chopped
1 (4-ounce) can mushrooms, drained
2 tablespoons butter
1/3 cup walnut halves
2 hard-cooked eggs, peeled and diced

Cook the onion and mushrooms in the butter in a skillet until golden brown. Place the onion mixture in a blender or food processor container. Add the walnuts and hard-cooked eggs. Process until smooth. Serve with crackers.

Serves Six to Eight

Shrimp Mold

8 ounces cream cheese
1/2 cup mayonnaise
1/2 cup cream of mushroom soup
1 envelope unflavored gelatin
2 (4-ounce) cans shrimp, drained
3/4 cup diced cucumber
1/4 cup finely chopped onion
1/8 teaspoon celery seeds

Melt the cream cheese in the top of a double boiler over hot water. Add the mayonnaise and mushroom soup. Cook until the mixture is blended and hot, stirring frequently. Soften the gelatin in a small amount of cold water. Add the gelatin mixture to the hot mixture, stirring until it is completely dissolved. Remove from the heat. Stir in the shrimp, cucumber, onion and celery seeds. Pour into a greased 1-quart mold. Refrigerate, covered, for 8 to 10 hours. Serve with crackers.

Serves Twelve

ARIZONA
BUILDING

Slow-Cooked Apple Butter

9 cups applesauce
5 cups sugar
¹/₂ cup packed brown sugar
¹/₄ cup vinegar
1 tablespoon cinnamon
¹/₄ teaspoon nutmeg
¹/₈ teaspoon ground cloves

Combine the applesauce, sugar, brown sugar, vinegar, cinnamon, nutmeg and cloves in a slow cooker, mixing well. Cover the cooker, placing a double thickness of paper towels under the lid to prevent the condensation from dripping into the apple mixture. Bring to a boil over high heat. Cook over low heat for 12 hours or until thick. Spoon into sterilized canning jars and seal.

Makes Ten Half-Pints

The Value of a Smile

A smile creates happiness in the home, fosters good will in business, and is the countersign to friends.

It is rest to the weary, daylight to the discouraged, sunshine to the sad, and nature's best antidote for trouble.

Yet it cannot be bought, begged, borrowed or stolen; for it is something that is no earthly good to anyone until it can be given away.

And if someone is too tired to give you a smile, just give them one of yours; for nobody needs a smile as much as those who have none left to give.

Baked Fruit Fiesta

1/2 to 3/4 cup cornflake crumbs
1 (16-ounce) jar applesauce
1 (15-ounce) can whole apricots, drained
1 (15-ounce) can whole plums, drained
1 (14-ounce) can sliced peaches, drained
1 (14-ounce) can sliced pears, drained
1 (14-ounce) can pineapple chunks,
    drained
1 (8-ounce) can green grapes, drained
Grated peel of 1 lemon (2 teaspoons)
2 tablespoons brown sugar
2 tablespoons honey
1/2 cup lemon juice

Cover the bottom of a 9x13-inch baking dish with about half the cornflake crumbs. Top with half the applesauce.

Add the apricots, plums, peaches, pears, pineapple and grapes in layers or combine the fruit and spoon over the applesauce in the baking dish. Sprinkle the lemon peel over the fruit.

Combine the brown sugar, honey and remaining applesauce in a bowl. Spoon evenly over the fruit. Drizzle with the lemon juice. Sprinkle the remaining cornflake crumbs over the top.

Bake at 350 degrees for 30 minutes or until hot and bubbly.

Serves Eight to Ten

Tropical Fruit Salsa

1 ripe mango, peeled and diced
1 cup diced fresh pineapple
1 cup diced honeydew melon
$1/2$ cup diced red bell pepper
$1/3$ cup rice wine vinegar
2 tablespoons minced fresh cilantro
$1/2$ teaspoon crushed red pepper

Combine the mango, pineapple, honeydew melon, red bell pepper, wine vinegar, cilantro and crushed red pepper in a bowl. Stir to mix well.

Refrigerate, covered, until chilled. Serve with tortilla chips.

Makes About Four Cups

Volunteer Services Department Mission Statement

Under the guidance of the President, the Auxiliary functions to achieve these objectives:

1. *To provide Tucson Medical Center with Volunteers, serving with special care and compassion.*
2. *Commitment to keeping our organization financially strong to support Tucson Medical Center's special needs by purchasing medical and building equipment.*
3. *To promote good will and mutual understanding between Tucson Medical Center and the community.*

Cactus Jelly

1 quart cactus pears (prickly pears)
1 (2-ounce) package powdered fruit
   pectin
3¹/₂ cups sugar
3 tablespoons lemon or lime juice

Brush the cactus pears with a vegetable brush. Rinse under running water. Place in a large saucepan with just enough water to cover. Bring to a boil. Boil until the pears are very tender and soft. Strain the pear mixture through a double thickness of cheesecloth or filter paper into a bowl. Let stand until any sediment settles to the bottom. Spoon the juice into a large saucepan; discard the sediment. (There should be 2¹/₂ cups juice.) Stir the pectin into the juice. Bring to a boil over high heat, stirring constantly. Stir in the sugar and lemon juice. Return to a rolling boil. Boil for 3 minutes. Remove from the heat. Skim and discard any surface foam. Pour into sterilized half-pint canning jars and seal with melted paraffin.

Note: For best results, do not substitute liquid pectin for powdered pectin. Include some underripe cactus pears as they have a higher pectin content. Do not double this recipe.

Makes Four or Five Half-Pints

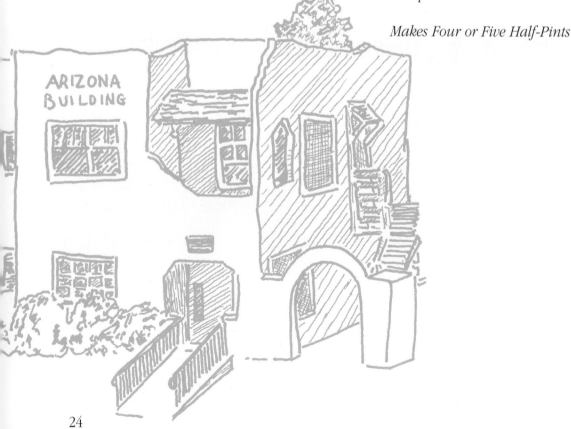

Out-of-this-World Pickles

7 cups thinly sliced cucumbers
3 cups thinly sliced onions
1 large green bell pepper, thinly sliced
4 cups sugar
2 cups vinegar
2 tablespoons celery seeds
1 tablespoon pickling salt

Combine the cucumbers, onions, green pepper, sugar, vinegar, celery seeds and pickling salt in a large saucepan.

Bring to a boil over medium-high heat. Boil until the sugar is dissolved. Remove from the heat. Let stand at room temperature for 2 hours.

Pack in sterilized jars or freezer containers. Refrigerate or freeze until ready to serve.

Makes Five Pints

The Surrey Service

Tucson Medical Center has a vast campus covering over forty acres and encompassing many buildings. It is a challenge for those in excellent physical condition to get around. In 1980, the TMC Auxiliary inaugurated a surrey service using a battery-powered vehicle staffed by a crew of male volunteers. Its purpose was to carry patients from the admitting area to the patient units. It soon became evident that there were greater transportation needs, and the service expanded to include the transport of employees and visitors as well as patients.

Today, two surreys, in radio contact with one another and a central staging area, can be found moving people all over the TMC campus. The well-trained drivers, male and female, are a gregarious lot who enjoy meeting people and being very busy.

The Desert Sanatorium

The Desert Sanatorium was at first just a dream of a young doctor. Bernard Wyatt, M.D. wanted a place to pursue his research into the benefits of sunlight on arthritis. It was already known to help tuberculosis patients. Where better than Arizona to find year-round sunshine and dry air?

The area he chose was Tucson, one of the oldest settlements in the United States. The tract of land, purchased at $25.00 an acre, was near old Fort Lowell, which had housed federal troops assigned to protect Tucson in its walled presidio during Apache Indian raids.

With considerable financial backing from Mr. and Mrs. Alfred Erickson of New York City, Dr. Wyatt and two partners formed a corporation to build a tuberculosis sanatorium. The partners withdrew, however, and left Dr. Wyatt with the project and the need for $40,000, a vast sum of money in those days. Again he managed to find backers and in November 1926 the Desert Sanatorium was opened with an administration building, president's residence, and four patient units of eight rooms each with a patio and great mountain views. The units, named Pima, Maricopa, Apache, and Navajo, had wicker furnishings and were decorated with Navajo rugs, southwestern art, and desert colors. A first-class chef provided gourmet meals. Evenings were given over to music recitals and well-known speakers. Many patients had private-duty nurses or attendants. Scientific research was carried on and the sanatorium developed a reputation as a luxury health resort with beautiful views, healing sun, and pure air.

Dr. Wyatt resigned in 1929 and Alfred Erickson assumed ownership of the facility. At his death in 1936, Mrs. Erickson continued to operate the sanatorium until the outbreak of World War II when civilian travel and wartime shortages of supplies and staff became major problems. She closed the facility in 1943, leaving only 350 hospital beds to serve the growing young city of 80,000. She offered to donate the 160 acres with buildings and equipment to the city of Tucson if funds could be raised to convert the Desert Sanatorium to a community hospital. The challenge was accepted and the Desert Sanatorium became Tucson Medical Center.

Breads & Brunch

Southwest Corn Bread

1 cup cornmeal
3/4 cup flour
1/3 cup sugar
1 tablespoon baking powder
1 cup milk
1 egg
1/2 (11-ounce) can niblet corn, drained
1/3 cup salsa
3 tablespoons corn oil
1 tablespoon diced jalapeño

Combine the cornmeal, flour, sugar and baking powder in a large bowl.

Whisk the milk, egg, corn, salsa, oil and jalapeño in a bowl until blended. Add to the cornmeal mixture. Stir just until mixed. Pour into a greased 8x8-inch baking pan.

Bake at 450 degrees for 25 to 30 minutes or until a wooden pick inserted in the center comes out clean. Cut into squares.

Serves Eight to Ten

Molasses Corn Bread

1/2 cup shortening
1/2 cup sugar
2 eggs
1 cup milk
1/2 cup molasses
1 cup sifted flour
1 tablespoon baking powder
1/2 teaspoon salt
1 1/2 cups unprocessed miller's bran
1/2 cup cornmeal

Cream the shortening and sugar in a large mixer bowl. Add the eggs 1 at a time, beating well after each addition. Stir in the milk and molasses.

Sift the flour, baking powder and salt into a bowl. Stir in the bran and cornmeal. Add to the creamed mixture and stir just until blended. Pour into a greased 9x9-inch baking pan.

Bake at 375 degrees for 30 minutes or until a wooden pick inserted in the center comes out clean. Cut into squares. Serve hot.

Serves Ten

Hopi Fry Bread (Weqiuir)

4 cups flour
5 teaspoons baking powder
1 1/2 teaspoons salt
2 to 2 1/4 cups water
Oil or melted shortening for deep-frying

Combine the flour, baking powder and salt in a large bowl. Stir in enough of the water, stirring to form a soft dough. Stir until the dough is smooth, shiny and no longer sticky to the touch, adding additional flour if necessary.

Cover the bowl with a towel and let stand at room temperature for 30 minutes. Shape the dough into 2 1/2-inch balls. Place on a lightly floured surface. Flatten each ball to a 1/2-inch thickness with a lightly floured rolling pin.

Pour oil into a large heavy pan to a 1 1/2-inch depth. Heat over medium-high heat until the oil is hot but not smoking. Add the flattened balls of dough a few at a time to the hot oil. Cook until browned on one side; turn over. Cook until browned on the other side.

Remove from the oil and drain on paper towels. Serve warm. May spread with honey, jelly or jam, sprinkle with confectioners' sugar or leave plain.

Note: Use folded bread rounds instead of taco shells as a fun way to serve tacos.

Serves Sixteen

Buddy's Grill Zucchini Muffins

30 eggs
6 pounds sugar
2 quarts cottonseed or vegetable oil
6 pounds grated zucchini
6 tablespoons vanilla extract
5$1/4$ pounds flour
2 tablespoons salt
2 tablespoons sifted baking soda
1$1/4$ teaspoons baking powder
6 tablespoons cinnamon
2 pounds shelled walnuts, coarsely
    chopped

Beat the eggs in a large bowl until light and foamy. Add the sugar, oil, zucchini and vanilla; mix well.

    Combine the flour, salt, baking soda, baking powder and cinnamon in a bowl. Add to the egg mixture and mix just until the dry ingredients are moistened. Stir in the walnuts.

    Pour equal amounts of the batter into greased or paper-lined muffin cups.

    Bake at 350 degrees for 12 to 15 minutes or until golden brown.

Note: For recipe success, it is important to add the ingredients in the order listed. May also bake the batter in greased 5x9-inch loaf pans.

Makes Twelve Dozen Muffins

Buddy's Grill

Rhubarb Muffins

1 cup buttermilk
$1/2$ cup vegetable oil
1 egg
1$1/4$ cups packed brown sugar
2 teaspoons vanilla extract
2$1/2$ cups flour
1 teaspoon baking soda
1 teaspoon baking powder
$1/2$ teaspoon salt
1$1/2$ cups diced fresh or frozen rhubarb
$1/2$ cup chopped walnuts
$1/3$ cup sugar
1 teaspoon cinnamon
1 teaspoon melted butter or margarine

Whisk the buttermilk, oil and egg in a large bowl until well blended. Add the brown sugar and vanilla and mix well.

    Combine the flour, baking soda, baking powder and salt in a bowl. Add to the buttermilk mixture and stir just until blended. Stir in the rhubarb and walnuts.

    Spoon the batter into 12 greased or paper-lined muffin cups, filling each cup $3/4$ full. Combine the sugar, cinnamon and butter in a bowl. Sprinkle over the muffin batter.

    Bake at 375 degrees for 20 to 25 minutes or until a wooden pick inserted in the centers comes out clean.

Makes Twelve Muffins

Banana Bread

¹/₂ cup shortening
1 cup sugar
2 eggs
1 cup mashed ripe bananas
1¹/₂ cups flour
1 teaspoon baking soda
¹/₄ teaspoon salt

Cream the shortening and sugar in a large mixer bowl until light and fluffy. Add the eggs 1 at a time, beating well after each addition. Beat in the bananas.

Sift the flour, baking soda and salt together. Add to the creamed mixture and mix until blended. Spoon the batter into a greased and floured 5x9-inch loaf pan.

Bake at 350 degrees for 1 hour or until a wooden pick inserted in the center comes out clean.

Cool in the pan on a wire rack for 10 minutes. Remove the loaf from the pan. Cool completely on a wire rack.

Serves Twelve

We never know what ripples
Of healing we set
In motion by simply smiling
On one another.

—Henry Drummond

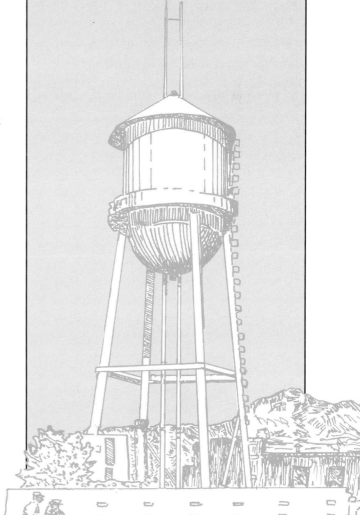

Hummingbird Bread

3 cups flour
2 cups sugar
1 teaspoon baking powder
1 teaspoon cinnamon
1/2 teaspoon salt
2 bananas, chopped
1 (8-ounce) can crushed pineapple
3 eggs, beaten
1 cup melted butter or vegetable oil
1 cup chopped walnuts or pecans
1 cup flaked coconut

Sift the flour, sugar, baking powder, cinnamon and salt into a large bowl. Combine the bananas, undrained pineapple, eggs and butter in a bowl and mix well.

Add to the flour mixture, stirring just until moistened. Stir in the walnuts and coconut. Pour the batter into a greased and floured 5x9-inch loaf pan.

Bake at 325 degrees for 1 1/4 hours or until a wooden pick inserted in the center comes out clean.

Cool in the pan on a wire rack for 10 minutes. Remove the loaf from the pan. Cool completely on a wire rack.

Note: May bake the bread in three 3x5-inch loaf pans. Bake for 20 to 30 minutes or until a wooden pick inserted in the centers comes out clean. Do not mash the bananas in this recipe.

Serves Twelve

Cranberry Nut Bread

2 cups flour
1 cup sugar
1 1/2 teaspoons baking powder
1/2 teaspoon baking soda
1/2 teaspoon salt
1 egg, beaten
2 tablespoons melted shortening
1/2 cup orange juice
2 teaspoons hot water
2 cups cranberries
1 cup chopped pecans

Combine the flour, sugar, baking powder, baking soda and salt in a large bowl.

Whisk the egg, shortening, orange juice and hot water in a bowl until well blended. Add to the flour mixture, stirring just until moistened.

Stir in the cranberries and pecans. Spoon the batter into a greased 5x9-inch loaf pan.

Bake at 350 degrees for 1 hour or until a wooden pick inserted in the center comes out clean.

Cool in the pan on a wire rack for 10 minutes. Remove the loaf from the pan. Cool completely on the wire rack.

Serves Twelve

Tucson Medical Center Patios

Unlike most hospitals, Tucson Medical Center is a one-level facility spread over many acres. This is a challenge when getting around but it is a blessing for the patients. Every room has a view of a patio, and patients and visitors favorably comment on this. Each patio is different but all have lovely plantings and offer a respite for patients and visitors alike. It is widely believed that the flowers, birds, and occasional small creatures have therapeutic value for patients.

One patio has been designated a hummingbird patio and was replanted with hummingbird-friendly flowers. Hummingbird feeders are also hung throughout the patio to supplement the little birds' energy needs. They are truly a joy to watch.

Pumpkin Bread

1²/₃ cups sifted flour
1 teaspoon baking soda
¹/₄ teaspoon baking powder
¹/₂ teaspoon cinnamon
¹/₂ teaspoon nutmeg
¹/₃ cup shortening
1¹/₃ cups sugar
2 eggs
1 cup mashed cooked pumpkin
1 teaspoon vanilla extract
¹/₃ cup cream sherry
¹/₂ cup chopped pecans (optional)

Sift the flour, baking soda, baking powder, cinnamon and nutmeg together.

Cream the shortening and sugar in a large mixer bowl until light and fluffy. Add the eggs 1 at a time, beating well after each addition. Mix in the pumpkin and vanilla.

Add the flour mixture alternately with the sherry, mixing well after each addition. Stir in the pecans. Pour the batter into a greased 5x9-inch loaf pan.

Bake at 350 degrees for 1 hour or until a wooden pick inserted in the center comes out clean.

Cool in the pan on a wire rack for 10 minutes. Remove the bread from the pan. Cool completely on the wire rack.

Wrap the bread tightly in plastic wrap and refrigerate.

Note: May also spoon the batter into paper-lined muffin cups, filling each cup ²/₃ full. Bake for 15 to 20 minutes or until a wooden pick inserted in the centers comes out clean.

Serves Twelve

Dilly Bread

1 envelope active dry yeast
$^{1}/_{4}$ cup warm water (105 to 115 degrees)
1 cup cottage cheese
1 tablespoon margarine
2 tablespoons sugar
2 tablespoons instant minced onion
$2^{1}/_{2}$ teaspoons dillseeds
1 teaspoon salt
$^{1}/_{4}$ teaspoon baking soda
1 egg
$2^{1}/_{4}$ cups flour
Melted butter

Dissolve the yeast in the warm water in a bowl. Heat the cottage cheese in a small saucepan over medium heat until warm. Place in a large mixer bowl.

Add the margarine and mix until melted. Beat in the sugar, onion, dillseeds, salt and baking soda. Blend in the dissolved yeast and egg.

Add the flour $^{1}/_{2}$ cup at a time, beating well after each addition. Cover the dough and let rise in a warm place for 1 hour or until doubled in bulk. Punch the dough down.

Place in a buttered $1^{1}/_{2}$- to 2-quart round baking dish. Let rise, covered, for 40 minutes.

Bake at 350 degrees for 40 to 50 minutes or until golden brown. Brush the top of the bread with melted butter and sprinkle lightly with additional salt.

Note: This bread is usually used as a sandwich loaf but is also delicious when served warm right from the oven.

Serves Eight to Ten

Lincoln Logs

4 to 5 cups flour
3/4 cup sugar
1 1/2 teaspoons salt
2 envelopes active dry yeast
1/2 cup milk
1/2 cup water
1/4 cup margarine
2 eggs, at room temperature
8 ounces cream cheese, softened
1 egg yolk
Chocolate frosting
1/3 cup chopped pecans

Combine 1 1/4 cups of the flour, 1/2 cup of the sugar, salt and yeast in a large mixer bowl. Place the milk, water and margarine in a small saucepan. Cook over low heat until warmed. (The margarine does not need to melt.)

Add to the yeast mixture; beat at medium speed for 2 minutes, occasionally scraping the side of the bowl. Add 1/2 cup of the remaining flour and mix well. Add the 2 eggs and beat at high speed for 2 minutes.

Stir in enough of the remaining flour to make a soft dough. Knead the dough on a floured surface for 8 to 10 minutes or until the dough is no longer sticky to the touch.

Place the dough in a greased bowl; cover. Let rise in a warm place for 1 hour or until doubled in bulk. Punch the dough down and divide into halves. Roll out each half to a 10x14-inch rectangle.

Beat the cream cheese with the remaining 1/4 cup sugar and egg yolk in a small bowl until light and fluffy. Spread half the cream cheese mixture evenly onto each rectangle. Roll each rectangle jelly roll fashion, starting at a short end. Press the edges together to seal.

Place the dough on a greased baking sheet. Cut slits 3/4 of the way into the dough at 1-inch intervals using a sharp knife. Cover and let rise in a warm place for 1 hour or until doubled in bulk.

Bake at 350 degrees for 20 to 25 minutes or until the bread sounds hollow when tapped. Remove to wire racks to cool completely.

Frost the cooled logs with chocolate frosting and sprinkle with the pecans.

Note: Use your favorite homemade chocolate frosting recipe or purchase canned chocolate frosting.

Serves Sixteen

The Water Tower

When the decision was made in 1926 to build the Desert Sanatorium, the first order of business was to provide an available water supply. A well was dug and a water tower erected. The water tower in the desert became a landmark to point the way to the hospital.

In 1986, a celebration was held to recognize the 60th anniversary of the silver tower. In time, it was no longer needed to store water and the tower was scheduled for demolition. "Old timers" rescued it by finding a new use for the tower. It took on new life as housing for Tucson Medical Center's transmission antenna.

This antenna serves the hospital paging system. Plant Services has kept the tower in good condition all through the years and it still stands proudly as a symbol of early Tucson and a TMC treasure.

Orange Bow Knots

1 envelope active dry yeast
$1/4$ cup warm water (105 to 115 degrees)
1 cup hot scalded milk
$1/2$ cup shortening
$1/3$ cup sugar
1 teaspoon salt
5 cups flour
2 eggs, beaten
2 tablespoons grated orange peel
$1/4$ cup orange juice
1 cup confectioners' sugar
1 teaspoon grated orange peel
2 tablespoons orange juice

Dissolve the yeast in the warm water in a bowl. Combine the milk, shortening, sugar and salt in a large mixer bowl. Mix until the shortening is melted. Let cool to lukewarm.

Beat in about 2 cups of the flour. Add the eggs 1 at a time, mixing well after each addition. Blend in the dissolved yeast. Add the 2 tablespoons orange peel, $1/4$ cup orange juice and enough of the remaining flour to make a soft dough. Cover and let stand for 10 minutes.

Knead on a lightly floured surface for 8 minutes or until smooth and elastic. Place the dough in a greased bowl and lightly grease the top of the dough. Cover and let rise in a warm place for 2 hours or until doubled in bulk. Punch the dough down and let rest for about 10 minutes.

Roll out the dough on a lightly floured surface with a lightly floured rolling pin to a 10x18-inch rectangle, about $1/2$ inch thick. Cut crosswise into eighteen $3/4$-inch-wide strips. Roll each strip between your fingers to form a rope. Tie each rope loosely into a knot. Place the knots on lightly greased baking sheets. Let rise for 45 minutes or until doubled in bulk.

Bake at 400 degrees for 12 minutes or until golden brown. Remove to wire racks to cool completely.

Combine the confectioners' sugar, 1 teaspoon orange peel and 2 tablespoons orange juice in a bowl and mix well. Dip the tops of the rolls into the frosting and let stand until set.

Makes Eighteen Rolls

Apple Ring Coffee Cake

3 cups flour
1¹/₂ cups sugar
1 teaspoon salt
1 teaspoon baking soda
1 teaspoon cinnamon
2 eggs, beaten
1 cup vegetable oil
2 teaspoons vanilla extract
2 Granny Smith apples, finely chopped
1 cup chopped walnuts
Confectioners' sugar

Combine the flour, sugar, salt, baking soda
and cinnamon in a large bowl. Whisk the
eggs, oil and vanilla in a bowl until well
blended. Add to the flour mixture. Stir just
until moistened.

Stir in the apples and walnuts. Spoon the
batter into a greased bundt pan.

Bake at 325 degrees for 1 hour or until a
wooden pick inserted in the center of the
coffee cake comes out clean.

Cool in the pan on a wire rack for
10 minutes. Remove from the pan. Cool
completely on the wire rack. Sprinkle lightly
with confectioners' sugar.

Serves Twelve

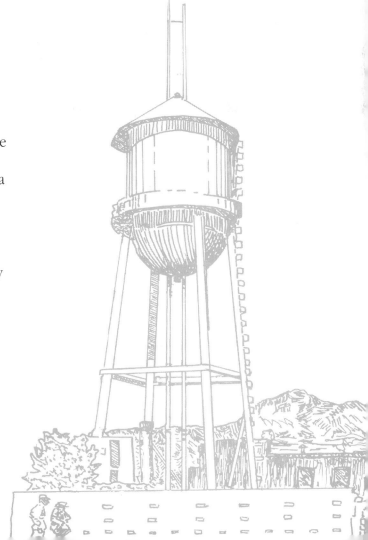

Palo Verde Hospital

When Tucson Medical Center opened, the need for a psychiatric hospital was recognized. The nearest facility was in Phoenix, which meant a long trip for patients and family members.

Many plans were suggested but all failed to materialize. This was most often due to insufficient funds. Still, in 1955, four patient rooms and a waiting area were provided in the Patio Building for electroshock therapy. This was a rudimentary beginning.

After much planning, construction began in 1983 on Palo Verde Hospital on the TMC campus. The new hospital opened in 1984 with sixty-two beds, eighteen of them for children and teenagers. The building was designed to look pleasing, not institutional.

TMC provided education programs, security, laboratory services, laundry, a medical library, employee health services, and use of radiology and clinic facilities. In return, Palo Verde was available for psychiatric consultations, most notably in the Restorative Services Department.

Reorganization took place in 1990 with an added emphasis on outpatient and outreach services. In 1993, Palo Verde became an integral and official arm of Tucson Medical Center. It continues to serve Tucson and the surrounding areas with the latest treatments and mental health programs.

Blueberry Brunch Cake

1/2 cup butter, softened
8 ounces cream cheese, softened
1 1/4 cups sugar
2 eggs
1 teaspoon vanilla extract
2 cups flour
1 teaspoon baking powder
1/2 teaspoon baking soda
1/4 teaspoon salt
1/2 cup milk
1 cup blueberries
1/2 cup packed brown sugar
1/2 cup flour
1 teaspoon cinnamon
3 tablespoons cold butter

Cream the 1/2 cup butter, cream cheese and sugar in a large mixer bowl until light and fluffy. Add the eggs 1 at a time, beating well after each addition. Add the vanilla, stirring until blended.

Sift the 2 cups flour, baking powder, baking soda and salt into a bowl. Add the sifted ingredients to the creamed mixture alternately with the milk, mixing well after each addition. Stir in the blueberries. Spread the batter in a buttered 9x13-inch baking pan.

Combine the brown sugar, 1/2 cup flour and cinnamon in a medium bowl. Cut in the 3 tablespoons butter until the mixture forms coarse crumbs. Sprinkle the crumb topping over the coffee cake batter.

Bake at 350 degrees for 30 to 35 minutes or until a wooden pick inserted in the center comes out clean. Cool on a wire rack.

Serves Twelve

A Growing Tucson

Tucson population has exploded in recent years. Evo De Concini, member of an old Tucson family, had the following recollection: "I recall very well when the Chamber of Commerce predicted that Tucson would be 50,000 people. I thought, 'That would be nice' but I didn't believe it. When we got 50,000, they said it was going to be 100,000 and I said, 'Now I know that will never be.' But in time it happened, and from then on I would believe any figure projected. It is now predicted by the Hudson Company of New York … that Tucson in the year 2012 will be 1,250,000 and now I believe it."

Quick Coffee Cake

1½ cups flour
½ cup sugar
2 teaspoons baking powder
¼ cup cold butter
1 egg, beaten
⅔ cup milk
1½ tablespoons melted butter
¼ cup sugar
1 tablespoon flour
½ teaspoon cinnamon

Sift the 1½ cups flour, ½ cup sugar and baking powder into a large bowl. Cut in the ¼ cup butter until the mixture forms coarse crumbs.

Whisk the egg and milk in a bowl until well blended. Add to the flour mixture and mix well. Spread the batter in a greased 9x9-inch baking pan. Brush the top with the melted butter.

Combine the ¼ cup sugar, 1 tablespoon flour and cinnamon in a bowl and mix well. Sprinkle over the coffee cake batter.

Bake at 400 degrees for 25 to 30 minutes or until a wooden pick inserted in the center comes out clean. Cool on a wire rack.

Serves Eight

Oatmeal Pancakes

1 cup rolled oats
1 1/2 cups buttermilk
2 eggs
3 tablespoons vegetable oil
1/2 cup flour
1/4 cup sugar
2 teaspoons baking powder
1/4 teaspoon baking soda
1/4 teaspoon salt

Combine the oats and buttermilk in a bowl. Refrigerate, covered, for 8 to 10 hours.

Whisk the eggs and oil in a large bowl until well blended.

Combine the flour, sugar, baking powder, baking soda and salt in a bowl. Add to the egg mixture and mix well. Stir in the oat mixture.

Spoon about 2 tablespoons of the batter onto a hot griddle or skillet for each pancake. Bake until golden brown on both sides, turning once.

Serves Four

Cancer Care Center of Southern Arizona

Tucson Medical Center has long had the largest cancer program in Arizona. In April 1993, the Cancer Care Center of Southern Arizona was officially opened in a 39,000-square-foot building on the TMC campus. Cancer patients and their families are offered complete services at CCCSA including radiation oncology, medical oncology, gynecological oncology, CT scanning, regular radiology, mammography, laboratory services, educational workshops, diet and nutritional counseling, social services, and support groups. The TMC Registry Service is located here, with tumor registry services offered to other hospitals and clinics throughout Arizona. Clinical research projects are ongoing and the CCCSA works closely with the Hospice program to further benefit patients. A resource library with books, brochures, audio and videotapes, and literature is available to patients and families. A special program is "Well Beauty" in which women patients receiving treatment are given wigs and taught ways to use scarves and decorative head wraps. They are also taught make-up tips to make them feel as attractive as they truly are. CCCSA with its marvelously warm and friendly staff is a TMC treasure.

Cornmeal Waffles

1¹/₄ cups flour
¹/₂ cup cornmeal
2 tablespoons sugar
2 teaspoons baking powder
¹/₂ teaspoon salt
3 egg yolks
1¹/₄ cups milk or buttermilk
2 tablespoons melted margarine
3 egg whites
Vegetable oil
1 cup chopped pecans or pine nuts

Combine the flour, cornmeal, sugar, baking powder and salt in a large bowl.

Whisk the egg yolks, milk and margarine in a bowl until well blended. Stir into the flour mixture.

Beat the egg whites in a small mixer bowl at high speed until stiff peaks form. Fold into the batter.

Brush a hot waffle iron with oil and sprinkle with about ¹/₄ cup of the pecans. Add about ¹/₂ cup of the batter. Bake until golden brown, turning once. Repeat with the remaining pecans and batter.

Serves Four or Five

Stuffed French Toast for Four

16 ounces cream cheese, softened
1/2 cup orange marmalade
1 loaf French bread
4 eggs, beaten
1 tablespoon sugar
1/4 teaspoon vanilla extract
1/8 teaspoon nutmeg
1 tablespoon butter
Maple syrup

Combine the cream cheese and marmalade in a bowl. Cut the bread crosswise into eight 1½-inch-thick slices. Cut a pocket in the side of each bread slice, being careful to not cut all the way through.

Fill a pastry bag with the cream cheese mixture and pipe evenly into the bread pockets.

Whisk the eggs, sugar, vanilla and nutmeg in a shallow dish until well blended. Dip the bread slices in the egg mixture, turning to coat both sides.

Melt the butter in a large skillet over medium heat. Add the bread slices. Cook until golden brown on both sides. Serve with maple syrup.

Serves Four

Tanque Verde Guest Ranch
Mark Shelton, Executive Chef

Tucson Medical Center Foundation

As TMC grew, it soon became apparent that a special organization was needed to manage fund-raising. Too many items and services were needed that weren't covered by regular revenues.

In 1980, a development committee was formed to devise a program to obtain funds from corporations, individuals, and foundations. This quickly became a success and the donor list grew rapidly. The TMC Foundation Board of Trustees was soon named. In just four years, the Foundation became a separate philanthropic organization. Specialists headed annual fund drives and special events and developed criteria for estate planning, raising millions of dollars. The Foundation supports over fifty special programs, including Oncology, Cardiology, Hospice, Education, and Palo Verde Behavioral Sciences programs.

In 1986, the TMC Foundation joined 125 other hospitals nationwide to take part in the Children's Miracle Network Telethon. It is a prime fund-raiser and every dollar given in Tucson and surrounding areas stays in Tucson. These dollars provide new furniture, expensive equipment, and funds for special needs to TMC's Pediatrics Department.

Overnight French Toast

3 eggs
$1/2$ cup milk
1 teaspoon vanilla extract
$1/2$ teaspoon almond extract
2 tablespoons sugar
$1/8$ teaspoon baking powder
6 slices Italian bread
$1/4$ cup butter or margarine
Maple syrup

Whisk the eggs with the milk and vanilla and almond flavorings in a bowl until well blended. Blend in the sugar and baking powder.

Place the bread slices in a single layer in a glass baking dish. Pour the egg mixture over the bread.

Cover the baking dish with plastic wrap. Refrigerate for 8 to 10 hours.

Melt the butter in a large skillet over medium heat. Add the bread slices. Bake until golden brown on both sides, turning once. Serve with hot maple syrup.

Serves Three

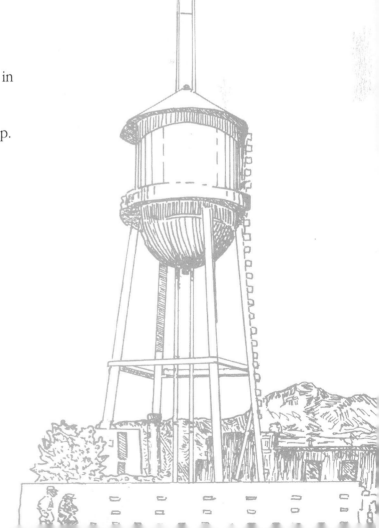

Caramel Apple Breakfast Pudding

2 large tart apples, such as Jonathan or
    Granny Smith
1/4 cup water
3/4 teaspoon cinnamon
1/2 cup packed brown sugar
2 tablespoons light corn syrup
2 tablespoons margarine or butter
1/4 cup pecan pieces
3 eggs, beaten
1 1/4 cups milk
1 teaspoon vanilla extract
1/4 teaspoon nutmeg
8 to 10 Italian or French bread slices,
    cut 1/2 inch thick

Peel, core and slice the apples. Place the apple slices and water in a small saucepan. Bring to a boil over high heat; reduce the heat to medium-low. Cook, covered, for 5 to 7 minutes or until the apples are tender, stirring occasionally. Drain the apples in a colander and place in a bowl. Add the cinnamon, tossing lightly to coat.

Combine the brown sugar, corn syrup and margarine in the same saucepan. Cook over medium heat until the mixture comes to a boil, stirring frequently. Remove from the heat. Pour into an 8x8-inch baking pan and sprinkle with the pecans.

Whisk the eggs, milk, vanilla and nutmeg in a bowl until well blended. Layer half the bread slices over the pecans in the baking dish, trimming the bread slices to fit if necessary. Top with the apple mixture and the remaining bread slices. Pour the egg mixture over the bread. Press the bread slices into the egg mixture to moisten completely.

Cover with plastic wrap. Refrigerate for 3 to 24 hours. Remove the plastic wrap.

Bake at 325 degrees for 40 to 45 minutes or until a knife inserted in the center comes out clean. Remove from the oven. Run a knife around the edges to loosen. Let stand for 15 minutes. Invert the pudding carefully onto a serving platter. Spoon any remaining caramel mixture in the dish over the pudding. Serve warm or cool.

Serves Eight

Special Easter Egg Casserole

12 eggs
2 cups sour cream
1 (4-ounce) can chopped green chiles
2 cups shredded Cheddar cheese
2 cups shredded Monterey Jack cheese

Whisk the eggs in a large bowl until foamy. Add the sour cream and chiles and mix well.

Stir in the Cheddar and Monterey Jack cheeses. Spoon the mixture into an 8x12-inch baking dish.

Bake at 350 degrees for 30 minutes or until the egg mixture is set in the center.

Note: May decrease the chiles used to 2 tablespoons for a milder flavor.

Serves Eight

Baked Chiles Rellenos

8 to 10 whole green chiles, fresh or
    canned
8 ounces Monterey Jack cheese
1¹/₂ cups shredded Cheddar cheese
3 eggs
1 cup milk
¹/₂ cup flour
2 teaspoons hot pepper sauce
¹/₄ teaspoon salt
¹/₄ teaspoon pepper

Cut a slit in 1 side of each of the chiles;
remove and discard the seeds.

Cut the Monterey Jack cheese into strips
to fit inside the slits in the chiles. Insert the
cheese strips into the chiles.

Place the chiles, cheese sides up, in a
greased 9x13-inch baking dish. Sprinkle with
the Cheddar cheese.

Whisk the eggs, milk and flour in a bowl
until well blended. Stir in the hot pepper
sauce, salt and pepper. Pour over the cheese.

Bake at 350 degrees for 30 to 45 minutes
or until a knife inserted in the center comes
out clean.

Serves Eight to Ten

Green Chiles and Cheese

1 (4-ounce) can whole green chiles,
    drained
2 cups shredded Cheddar cheese
2 cups shredded Monterey Jack cheese
4 to 5 eggs

Cut the chiles lengthwise into halves;
remove and discard the seeds.

Place the chiles, cut sides up, in a
greased 9-inch pie plate. Sprinkle with the
Cheddar and Monterey Jack cheeses.

Whisk the eggs in a bowl until foamy
and pour over the cheese. Cover the dish
with foil.

Bake at 350 degrees for 30 minutes.
Reduce the oven temperature to 250 degrees.
Bake, uncovered, for 10 minutes or until the
top is golden brown and a knife inserted in
the center comes out clean. Cut into wedges
to serve.

Note: May increase the chiles used to 2 cans
for additional flavor. Serve as a main dish
or appetizer.

Serves Eight

Cheesy Potato Casserole

1 (24- to 32-ounce) package frozen hash
    brown potatoes
2 cups sour cream
1 (10-ounce) can cream of mushroom
    soup
1/2 cup chopped onion
1/2 teaspoon salt
1/2 teaspoon pepper
2 cups shredded Cheddar cheese
1/2 cup melted margarine
2 cups cornflakes, slightly crushed

Break up the hash browns. Place in a
buttered 9x13-inch baking pan.

Combine the sour cream, soup, onion,
salt and pepper in a large bowl. Stir in the
cheese and 1/4 cup of the melted margarine.
Spoon over the potatoes.

Sprinkle with the cornflake crumbs.
Drizzle with the remaining 1/4 cup melted
margarine. Bake at 350 degrees for 1 hour.

Serves Twelve

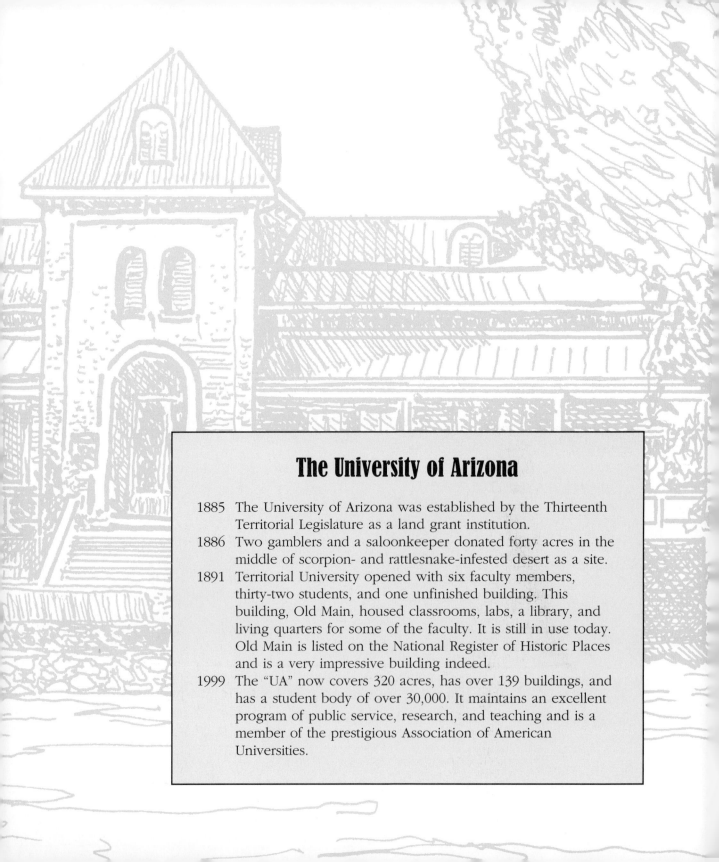

The University of Arizona

1885   The University of Arizona was established by the Thirteenth Territorial Legislature as a land grant institution.

1886   Two gamblers and a saloonkeeper donated forty acres in the middle of scorpion- and rattlesnake-infested desert as a site.

1891   Territorial University opened with six faculty members, thirty-two students, and one unfinished building. This building, Old Main, housed classrooms, labs, a library, and living quarters for some of the faculty. It is still in use today. Old Main is listed on the National Register of Historic Places and is a very impressive building indeed.

1999   The "UA" now covers 320 acres, has over 139 buildings, and has a student body of over 30,000. It maintains an excellent program of public service, research, and teaching and is a member of the prestigious Association of American Universities.

Soups

Chilled Cantaloupe Soup

*4 medium cantaloupes, halved and
  seeded*
1¹/₂ cups apple juice
²/₃ cup sugar
¹/₂ cup dry sherry
1 tablespoon lemon juice
³/₄ teaspoon ginger
³/₄ teaspoon vanilla extract

Scoop the cantaloupe pulp into a large
bowl. Wrap the cantaloupe shells in plastic
wrap. Refrigerate until ready to use.

Add the apple juice, sugar, sherry,
lemon juice, ginger and vanilla to the pulp,
stirring to combine. Process 2 cups of the
cantaloupe mixture at a time in a blender or
food processor container until smooth.

Pour into a bowl. Refrigerate, covered,
for 4 to 8 hours, stirring occasionally.

Serve in the reserved cantaloupe shells or
soup bowls. Garnish with fresh mint sprigs,
thin lime slices or whipped cream.

Serves Eight

Olé Gazpacho

3 medium tomatoes, peeled and diced
1 large cucumber, peeled and diced
1 large onion, diced
1 green bell pepper, diced
1 canned pimento, drained and diced
2 (12-ounce) cans tomato juice
1/3 cup olive oil
1/3 cup red wine vinegar
1 1/2 teaspoons salt
1/4 teaspoon Tabasco sauce
1/8 teaspoon coarsely ground pepper

Combine the tomatoes, cucumber, onion, green pepper, pimento, tomato juice, olive oil, vinegar, salt, Tabasco sauce and pepper in a bowl.

Process half the mixture at a time in a blender or food processor container until puréed. Pour into a bowl.

Refrigerate, covered, for 3 hours or until well chilled. Serve with croutons and garnish with chopped fresh chives.

Serves Six

Low-Fat Broccoli Soup

2 pounds broccoli with stems
   (about 5 cups)
1 medium yellow onion, chopped
   (about 1 1/2 cups)
2 teaspoons olive oil
3 garlic cloves, crushed
1 tablespoon flour
8 cups water
1 large baking potato, peeled and
   chopped (about 1 3/4 cups)
1 3/4 teaspoons salt
1/2 teaspoon thyme
1/4 teaspoon white pepper
1 (12-ounce) can evaporated skim milk
1 tablespoon lemon juice

Remove and reserve the florets from the broccoli. Peel and coarsely chop the broccoli stems; set aside.

Sauté the onion in the olive oil in a large saucepan for 3 to 4 minutes or until tender. Add the garlic. Sauté for 1 minute. Stir in the flour. Cook for 1 minute, stirring constantly. Add the water. Bring to a boil over low heat.

Stir in the potato, broccoli florets and stems, salt, thyme and white pepper. Simmer, covered, for 35 minutes. Stir in the evaporated milk and lemon juice.

Simmer, uncovered, for 15 minutes. Strain the soup, reserving the broth and vegetables separately. Purée the vegetables in a blender or food processor container. Stir the puréed vegetables into the broth. Serve immediately.

Serves Four to Six

Baked French Onion Soup

6 cups thinly sliced onions
1/4 teaspoon sugar
1/4 cup butter
3 (10-ounce) cans beef broth
3 broth cans water
2 tablespoons brandy (optional)
1/2 teaspoon salt
1/2 teaspoon pepper
6 slices French bread
Grated Parmesan cheese

Sprinkle the onions with the sugar. Cook the sugared onions in the butter in a large saucepan over low heat until golden brown, stirring occasionally. Stir in the broth and water.

Bring to a boil; reduce the heat to low. Simmer gently for 45 minutes. Stir in the brandy, salt and pepper.

Ladle the soup into 6 ovenproof soup bowls. Top each serving with a bread slice. Sprinkle desired amount of Parmesan cheese over the bread. Bake at 400 degrees for 8 minutes or until the cheese is melted.

Serves Six

Golden Cream of Potato Soup

6 cups cubed peeled potatoes
2 cups water
1 cup sliced celery
1 cup thinly sliced carrots
1/2 cup diced onion
2 chicken bouillon cubes
2 teaspoons parsley flakes
1 teaspoon salt
1/8 teaspoon pepper
3 cups milk
1/4 cup flour
12 ounces Cheddar cheese, cubed

Combine the potatoes, water, celery, carrots, onion, bouillon cubes, parsley flakes, salt and pepper in a large saucepan.

Bring to a boil; reduce the heat to low. Simmer, covered, for 8 to 10 minutes or until the vegetables are tender.

Stir 1/4 cup of the milk gradually into the flour in a small bowl, forming a smooth paste. Stir into the soup. Add the remaining 2 3/4 cups milk and the cheese.

Cook over medium heat until thickened and the cheese is completely melted.

Serves Four to Six

Tucson Trivia

Tucson flew the Confederate flag during the Civil War, but only for about three months in 1862. Union and Confederate troops engaged in a minor skirmish at Picacho Peak about forty miles northwest of Tucson. This represented the westernmost battle of the Civil War and ensured Tucson a place in the history books.

Simple Spinach Soup

1/4 cup chopped onion
1 garlic clove, minced (optional)
1 tablespoon butter or olive oil
1 (48-ounce) can chicken or beef broth
1/4 cup acini di pepe pasta
1 (10-ounce) package frozen chopped
    spinach, thawed
1/4 teaspoon nutmeg
1/8 teaspoon pepper
Salt to taste
Grated Parmesan cheese

Sauté the onion and garlic in the butter in a large saucepan until tender, but not browned. Add the chicken broth. Bring the mixture to a boil. Stir in the pasta, spinach, nutmeg and pepper.

Simmer for 5 minutes or until the pasta is tender, stirring occasionally. Season with salt. Sprinkle with Parmesan cheese. Serve hot.

Note: Recipe may be doubled and frozen for later use.

Serves Six

Gingered Squash and Veggie Soup

1 large onion, diced
2 tablespoons vegetable oil
1 teaspoon ginger
$^1/_2$ teaspoon salt
$^1/_2$ teaspoon cumin
$^1/_2$ teaspoon dry mustard
$^1/_4$ teaspoon mace
$^1/_4$ teaspoon cinnamon
$^1/_4$ teaspoon black pepper
$^1/_8$ teaspoon cayenne
6 cups cubed peeled butternut squash
    (about 2 pounds)
12 ounces cubed peeled sweet potato
$^3/_4$ cup thickly sliced parsnip
5 (10-ounce) cans chicken broth
1 cup 1% milk

Sauté the onion in the oil in a large saucepan for 2 minutes. Stir in the ginger, salt, cumin, dry mustard, mace, cinnamon, black pepper and cayenne.

Reduce the heat to low. Cook, covered, for 5 minutes. Add the squash, sweet potato, parsnip and chicken broth.

Bring to a boil; reduce the heat to low. Simmer, partially covered, for 30 minutes or until the vegetables are tender.

Purée the vegetables in batches in a blender or food processor container.

Return puréed vegetables to the saucepan. Stir in the milk. Cook, stirring occasionally, until heated through.

Serves Six to Eight

The Arizona Inn

Set on fourteen beautifully manicured acres in midtown Tucson, the Arizona Inn is Tucson's oldest resort, built in 1930 by Isabel Greenway, a multi-talented and very gracious lady. As a young widow with a family and an interest in politics and veteran's affairs, she moved to Tucson in 1927 where she established a furniture workshop to employ disabled veterans. Finding herself with a warehouse full of fine furniture and a failing national economy in 1930, Mrs. Greenway established the Arizona Inn as a logical way to utilize all that furniture. The Inn was an immediate success and has remained so until this day.

Well known for being painted an arresting shade of pink on the outside, the interior is very elegant and very subdued. With a deserved reputation for fine food, the Inn is the scene of parties and celebrations of every description. The lushly planted grounds, with an incredible array of flowers, are the scene of many weddings each year.

The rooms at the Inn still use the original furniture made some seventy years ago. Many people return annually for a short vacation or for the entire winter season. The Arizona Inn is always worth a visit.

Pasta Fazool

2 ounces salt pork, finely chopped
2 tablespoons olive oil
3 ribs celery, finely chopped
1 large onion, finely chopped
1 carrot, finely chopped
3 garlic cloves, finely chopped
1 tablespoon finely chopped parsley
1 cup tomato sauce
1/2 teaspoon salt
1/8 teaspoon pepper
3 quarts warm water
1 pound macaroni
2 (15-ounce) cans white beans
Grated Parmesan cheese

Sauté the salt pork in the heated olive oil in a large saucepan for 3 minutes. Add the celery, onion, carrot, garlic and parsley. Sauté until well browned. Stir in the tomato sauce, salt and pepper.

Cook for about 10 minutes, stirring frequently. Add the warm water. Bring to a boil. Cook for about 10 minutes. Stir in the pasta. Boil, uncovered, for 15 minutes or until the pasta is tender.

Add the undrained beans. Cook until heated through, stirring frequently to prevent the pasta from sticking to the pan. Serve hot topped with Parmesan cheese.

Serves Four to Six Generously

Easy Minestrone

1 onion, chopped
1 to 2 garlic cloves, chopped
1 tablespoon vegetable oil
4 cups assorted chopped vegetables
    (zucchini, carrots, spinach, Swiss
    chard, mushrooms)
1 (28-ounce) jar spaghetti sauce
1 to 2 (15-ounce) cans kidney beans,
    drained
1 cup small pasta shells, cooked and
    drained
Basil to taste
Oregano to taste
Salt and pepper to taste
1 to 2 (14-ounce) cans chicken broth

Sauté the onion and garlic in the oil in a large saucepan until tender. Add the desired vegetables. Cook until the vegetables are tender.

Stir in the spaghetti sauce, kidney beans, pasta, basil, oregano, salt and pepper. Add enough broth to make of desired consistency.

Bring to a boil. Reduce the heat to low. Simmer for 10 minutes.

Serves Six to Eight

Mexican Meatball Soup

1 pound ground beef
1 cup dry bread crumbs
1 onion, minced
6 tablespoons dry sherry
3/4 teaspoon salt
3/4 teaspoon chili powder
2 (10-ounce) cans beef consommé
2 soup cans water
1 bay leaf

Combine the ground beef, bread crumbs, onion, 1 tablespoon of the sherry, salt and chili powder in a bowl. Shape into 1-inch meatballs.

Place the consommé, water and bay leaf in a large saucepan. Bring to a boil. Add the meatballs a few at a time so the broth remains at a constant boil. Stir in the remaining 5 tablespoons sherry. Reduce the heat to low.

Simmer, covered, for about 30 minutes or until the meatballs are cooked through. Remove and discard the bay leaf before serving. Serve with cooked rice if desired.

Note: May substitute 4 beef bouillon cubes and 4 cups water for the beef consommé and soup cans of water.

Serves Four to Six

Beefed-Up Soup

1 pound ground beef
1 cup diced onion
1 garlic clove, crushed
1 (16-ounce) can whole tomatoes
3 cups water
1 cup red wine
1 (10-ounce) bag frozen corn
1 cup diced carrots
1 beef bouillon cube
2¹/₂ teaspoons salt
¹/₂ teaspoon thyme
2 tablespoons butter
2 tablespoons flour
¹/₂ cup milk

Brown the ground beef with the onion and garlic in a large saucepan, stirring until the ground beef is crumbly; drain.

Add the undrained tomatoes, water, wine, corn, carrots, bouillon cube, salt and thyme, stirring to break up the tomatoes.

Bring to a boil; reduce the heat to low. Simmer until the vegetables are tender, stirring occasionally. Skim off and discard any fat from the surface.

Melt the butter in a small saucepan. Add the flour, stirring until smooth. Add the milk gradually, stirring constantly until thickened.

Stir the milk mixture into the soup. Cook for 5 minutes or until heated through. Serve hot.

Note: May also add ¹/₂ cup chopped green bell pepper and/or ¹/₂ cup barley.

Serves Eight

The Garden of Gethsemane or Felix Lucero Park

As Felix Lucero, a World War I veteran, lay wounded on the battlefield, he vowed that if he survived he would devote twenty years of his life to God by creating religious statues.

Lucero arrived in Tucson in 1938 and began to fulfill his vow. He lived under the Congress Street Bridge near downtown and, using concrete, sand, and debris from the riverbed, began his construction project. He did this, of course, on land he didn't own, but in the western tradition of "live and let live," no one seemed to mind. Over the years, statues of the Last Supper, the Baby Jesus with Joseph and Mary, and Jesus on the cross and in the tomb took shape. These can be viewed free of charge and have served as an inspiration to residents and visitors alike.

Southwest Taco Soup

1¹/₂ pounds lean ground beef
1 (23-ounce) can ranch-style beans
1 (15-ounce) can pinto beans
1 (15-ounce) can kidney beans
1 (15-ounce) can corn, drained
1 (14-ounce) can Mexican-style tomatoes
1 large onion, chopped
3 ribs celery, chopped
2 (1-ounce) envelopes taco
   seasoning mix
1 (1-ounce) envelope ranch salad
   dressing mix

Brown the ground beef in a skillet, stirring until crumbly; drain.

Combine the browned beef, undrained ranch-style beans, undrained pinto beans, undrained kidney beans, corn, undrained tomatoes, onion and celery in a slow cooker and mix well. Stir in the taco seasoning mix and salad dressing mix.

Cook, covered, on Low for 8 hours.

Serves Ten

Chili Stew

1 cup sliced onion
2 medium green or red bell peppers,
   sliced
1 garlic clove, sliced
¹/₄ cup vegetable oil
1 pound ground beef
1 (15-ounce) can kidney beans
1 (15-ounce) can whole peeled tomatoes
1¹/₂ teaspoons salt
¹/₂ teaspoon black pepper
¹/₂ teaspoon celery salt
¹/₂ teaspoon chili powder, or to taste
¹/₈ teaspoon cayenne
¹/₈ teaspoon thyme
¹/₈ teaspoon marjoram

Sauté the onion, bell peppers and garlic in the oil in a large saucepan until tender. Add the ground beef. Cook until brown and crumbly; drain.

Stir in the undrained kidney beans, undrained tomatoes, salt, black pepper, celery salt, chili powder, cayenne, thyme and marjoram.

Bring to a boil; reduce the heat to low. Simmer for 30 minutes, stirring occasionally.

Serves Six to Eight

Speedy Chili

1 pound ground beef
1/2 cup chopped onion
1/2 cup chopped celery
1 (16-ounce) can stewed tomatoes
1 (15-ounce) can kidney beans
1 (10-ounce) can tomato soup
2 teaspoons chili powder
1 teaspoon salt
1/8 teaspoon pepper

Brown the ground beef with the onion and celery in a large saucepan, stirring until the ground beef is crumbly; drain. Stir in the undrained tomatoes, undrained kidney beans, tomato soup, chili powder, salt and pepper.

Bring to a boil; reduce the heat to low. Simmer, covered, for 20 minutes or until heated through. Top with shredded cheese if desired.

Note: May substitute 2 tablespoons instant minced onions for the 1/2 cup chopped onion. Add with the tomatoes.

Serves Six

Cowboy Beef and Beans

8 ounces ground beef
8 ounces bacon, chopped
1 medium onion, chopped
1 (28-ounce) can pork and beans
1 (15-ounce) can butter beans
1 (15-ounce) can kidney beans
1/2 cup packed brown sugar
1/2 cup vinegar
1/4 cup catsup
Salt and pepper to taste

Brown the ground beef with the bacon and onion in a skillet, stirring until the ground beef is crumbly; drain.

Combine the beef mixture, pork and beans, undrained butter beans, undrained kidney beans, brown sugar, vinegar and catsup in a slow cooker. Season with salt and pepper.

Cook on High for 3 hours, stirring occasionally.

Serves Six to Eight

Quick-and-Easy Mexican Soup

1 (26-ounce) can chicken broth
1 (15-ounce) can pinto beans
1 (15-ounce) can hominy
1 (10-ounce) can diced tomatoes with green chiles
8 ounces frozen cut okra
1 (1-ounce) envelope taco seasoning mix
1 (1-ounce) envelope ranch salad dressing mix
1 teaspoon onion powder
2 boneless skinless chicken breasts, cooked
Chicken broth

Combine 1 can chicken broth, undrained pinto beans, undrained hominy, tomatoes, okra, taco seasoning mix, salad dressing mix and onion powder in a large saucepan.

Bring to a boil; reduce the heat to low. Simmer until the seasoning mixes are thoroughly blended, stirring constantly.

Cut the chicken into bite-size pieces. Stir the chicken into the soup. Simmer for 20 minutes.

Stir in additional chicken broth if the soup is too thick. Garnish each serving with several tortilla chips.

Note: This soup freezes well.

Serves Six

Sausage Soup

1 pound bulk hot pork sausage
1 pound bulk mild pork sausage
1 quart water
1 (16-ounce) can whole peeled tomatoes
1 (15-ounce) can pinto beans
1 cup chopped onion
1/2 green bell pepper, chopped
1/2 teaspoon pepper
1/2 teaspoon garlic salt
1 bay leaf
1 1/2 cups diced potatoes

Brown the hot and mild sausages in a large saucepan, stirring until crumbly; drain. Stir in the water, undrained tomatoes, undrained pinto beans, onion, green pepper, pepper, garlic salt and bay leaf.

Bring to a boil; reduce the heat to low. Simmer for 1 hour, stirring occasionally.

Stir in the potatoes. Simmer until the potatoes are tender. Remove and discard the bay leaf before serving.

Serves Eight to Ten

Seafood Gumbo

1 (26-ounce) can chicken broth
1 (15-ounce) can Manhattan clam
     chowder
1 (10-ounce) can tomato soup
8 ounces frozen cut okra
5 ounces crab meat or imitation crab
     meat, flaked
5 ounces cooked baby shrimp
1/4 cup dry sherry or red wine
1 teaspoon onion powder
2 to 3 drops of Tabasco sauce or to taste

Combine the broth, chowder and tomato soup in a large saucepan. Add the okra, crab meat and shrimp and mix well. Stir in the sherry, onion powder and Tabasco sauce.

Bring to a boil; reduce the heat to low. Simmer for 30 minutes. Serve in bowls over cooked rice if desired.

Note: This soup freezes well. May substitute any canned seafood soup for the Manhattan clam chowder.

Serves Six

Savory Seafood Chowder

1 (8-ounce) can minced clams
1 (7-ounce) can crab meat
1 (4-ounce) can shrimp
4 slices bacon, diced
1 garlic clove, minced
2 cups diced potatoes
1 cup white wine
1/2 cup chopped green onions
2 teaspoons salt
1/2 teaspoon thyme
1/8 teaspoon pepper
1 (16-ounce) can cream-style corn
3 cups milk
1 cup light cream or half-and-half
2 tablespoons minced fresh parsley

Drain the clams, crab meat and shrimp, reserving the liquids. Slice the crab meat; set aside.

Sauté the bacon and garlic in a large saucepan until the bacon is crisp. Add the potatoes, wine, green onions, salt, thyme, pepper and reserved shellfish liquids.

Simmer, covered, for 15 to 20 minutes or until the potatoes are tender. Stir in the clams, crab meat, shrimp, corn, milk, cream and parsley. Heat over low heat until simmering. Do not boil. Serve with French bread if desired.

Serves Eight

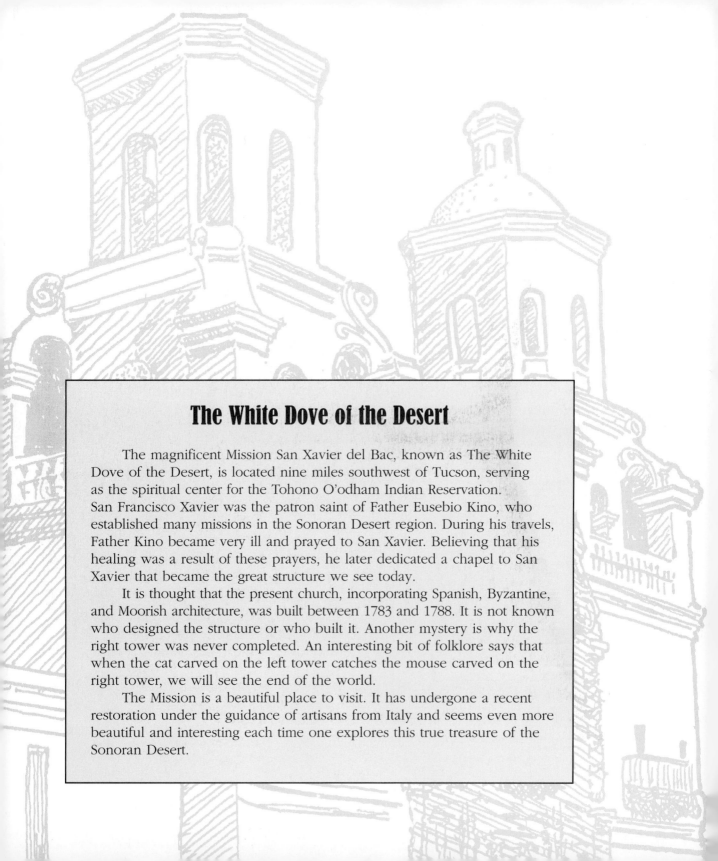

The White Dove of the Desert

The magnificent Mission San Xavier del Bac, known as The White Dove of the Desert, is located nine miles southwest of Tucson, serving as the spiritual center for the Tohono O'odham Indian Reservation. San Francisco Xavier was the patron saint of Father Eusebio Kino, who established many missions in the Sonoran Desert region. During his travels, Father Kino became very ill and prayed to San Xavier. Believing that his healing was a result of these prayers, he later dedicated a chapel to San Xavier that became the great structure we see today.

It is thought that the present church, incorporating Spanish, Byzantine, and Moorish architecture, was built between 1783 and 1788. It is not known who designed the structure or who built it. Another mystery is why the right tower was never completed. An interesting bit of folklore says that when the cat carved on the left tower catches the mouse carved on the right tower, we will see the end of the world.

The Mission is a beautiful place to visit. It has undergone a recent restoration under the guidance of artisans from Italy and seems even more beautiful and interesting each time one explores this true treasure of the Sonoran Desert.

Salads

Frozen Fruit Cups

1¼ cups orange juice
1 cup water
1 small package orange gelatin
½ cup sugar
½ cup lemon juice
2 medium bananas, mashed

Combine the orange juice and water in a medium saucepan. Bring to a boil.

Pour over the gelatin in a medium bowl and stir until the gelatin is dissolved.

Stir in the sugar and lemon juice until the sugar is dissolved. Add the bananas and mix well.

Divide the mixture evenly among twelve 6-ounce plastic cups or freezerproof dessert dishes. Freeze until firm.

Garnish with fresh orange slices or dollops of whipped cream.

Note: If freezing the salads in plastic cups, use a double layer of cups.

Serves Twelve

Molded Apricot Salad

1 (20-ounce) can crushed pineapple
2 (16-ounce) cans apricots
1 large or 2 small packages apricot
    gelatin
2 cups sour cream
1 envelope unflavored gelatin
½ cup cold water

Drain the pineapple and apricots, reserving the juices; mash the apricots. Add enough water to the reserved juices to measure 3 cups. Pour into a medium saucepan. Bring to a boil.

Place the apricot gelatin in a large bowl. Add the hot juice mixture, stirring until the gelatin is dissolved. Add the apricots to the apricot gelatin mixture along with the pineapple and sour cream and mix well.

Soften the unflavored gelatin in the cold water. Add to the pineapple mixture and mix well. Pour the gelatin mixture into a lightly greased 2-quart mold. Refrigerate, covered, until firm. Unmold onto a serving plate.

Serves Eight

Festive Cranberry Salad

1 (12-ounce) package fresh cranberries
1 large orange or 2 medium seedless
   oranges with peel, cut into chunks
2 small packages cranberry or cherry
   gelatin
2 cups boiling water
2 cups sugar
2 envelopes unflavored gelatin
1/2 cup cold water
1 (20-ounce) can crushed pineapple
1 cup chopped celery
1 cup chopped pecans

Place the cranberries and orange in a food
processor container. Process until coarsely
ground.

Dissolve the cranberry gelatin in the
boiling water in a bowl. Stir in the sugar.
Refrigerate until partially set. Soften the
unflavored gelatin in the cold water. Add to
the cranberry gelatin and mix well.

Stir in the ground cranberry mixture,
undrained pineapple, celery and pecans.
Pour into a 2-quart ring mold. Refrigerate
until firm. Unmold onto a serving plate.

Serves Eight

Sabino Canyon

An oasis has been described as serving as a pleasant relief, refuge, or change from the usual, the annoying, or the difficult. This certainly characterizes Sabino Canyon recreation area located at the northeastern edge of Tucson. A beautiful combination of mountains, water, and valley, Sabino Canyon attracts more than a million visitors a year. They come to enjoy the desert sun, the tranquility of flowing water, and a wide variety of plants and animals. Trails of diverse difficulty are available for strollers and hikers. A three and seven-eighths mile road built by the Civil Conservation Corps in the 1930s provides access to upper Sabino Canyon. For the exercise-challenged, trams provide access to this area on a regular schedule and are accompanied by informative narrative. Trams also make scheduled runs to Lower Bear Canyon, where a two and one-half mile trail leads to Seven Falls, a beautiful area well worth the effort to get to. Sabino Canyon is a treasure of the Sonoran Desert, appreciated by all who are fortunate enough to visit once or, like Tucsonans, many times.

Fresh Broccoli Salad

1 large bunch broccoli
1 pound turkey bacon, cooked and crumbled
1/2 medium red onion, chopped
1 cup sunflower kernels
1/2 cup sliced fresh mushrooms
1/2 cup raisins
1 cup mayonnaise
1/4 cup sugar
2 tablespoons cider vinegar

Cut the broccoli florets and tender stalks into bite-size pieces. Combine the broccoli, bacon, onion, sunflower kernels, mushrooms and raisins in a large bowl and mix lightly.

Blend the mayonnaise, sugar and vinegar in a bowl. Add to the broccoli mixture, tossing gently until the broccoli mixture is evenly coated with the mayonnaise mixture. Refrigerate, covered, for 2 to 4 hours or until chilled.

Note: If using salted sunflower kernels, rinse the salt from the kernels before adding to the salad.

Serves Four to Six

Mandarin Salad

1/4 cup slivered almonds
4 teaspoons sugar
1/4 head iceberg lettuce
1/4 head romaine
2 ribs celery, diagonally sliced
2 green onions with tops, sliced
1/4 cup vegetable oil
2 tablespoons sugar
2 tablespoons vinegar
1 tablespoon minced fresh parsley
1/2 teaspoon salt
1/8 teaspoon pepper
Tabasco sauce to taste
1 (11-ounce) can mandarin orange
    sections, drained

Place the almonds and 4 teaspoons sugar in a small skillet. Cook over low heat until the sugar is melted and the almonds are evenly coated, stirring constantly. Remove from the heat. Cool the almonds; break apart.

Tear the iceberg lettuce and romaine into bite-size pieces. Place in a large sealable plastic bag. Add the celery and green onions and toss to mix.

Whisk the oil, 2 tablespoons sugar, vinegar, parsley, salt, pepper and Tabasco sauce in a bowl until well blended. Add to the lettuce mixture along with the oranges. Seal the bag. Shake until the salad ingredients are evenly coated with the dressing.

Note: Before the dressing and oranges are added, the bagged salad can be refrigerated for up to 24 hours.

Serves Four to Six

Hot Potato Salad with White Wine

2¹/₂ pounds potatoes
¹/₃ cup dry white wine
¹/₂ cup peanut or olive oil
Salt and freshly ground pepper to taste

Rinse the potatoes. Place in a 3-quart saucepan. Add enough cold water to cover the potatoes.

Bring to a boil. Simmer for 20 minutes or until the potatoes are tender. Do not overcook the potatoes.

Drain the potatoes; cool slightly. Peel the potatoes and cut into ¹/₄-inch-thick slices. Place in a large ovenproof bowl.

Add the wine, oil, salt and pepper, tossing lightly. Cover with foil.

Bake at 200 degrees until heated through. Serve warm.

Serves Eight to Ten

Orange and Black Bean Salad

8 ounces dried black beans
4 cups water
2 seedless oranges, peeled and cut into bite-size pieces
1 cup coarsely chopped red bell pepper
¹/₂ cup sliced celery
¹/₂ cup sliced green onions
¹/₃ cup coarsely chopped cilantro leaves
¹/₄ cup freshly squeezed orange juice
4¹/₂ teaspoons olive oil
¹/₄ teaspoon salt

Rinse and sort the beans. Place in a large saucepan. Add the water. Bring to a boil. Simmer, loosely covered, over medium-low heat for 1¹/₂ hours or until the beans are tender, stirring occasionally. Drain the beans; cool. (You should have about 3 cups cooked beans.)

Place the beans in a large bowl. Add the oranges, red pepper, celery, green onions and cilantro and toss lightly.

Combine the orange juice, oil and salt in a bowl. Stir into the bean mixture. Refrigerate, covered, for 3 to 4 hours or until chilled.

Serves Eight

Southwestern Caesar Salad with Chipotle Dressing

2 large ears of corn, unhusked
*2 heads romaine lettuce, torn into bite-
    size pieces*
4 plum tomatoes, peeled and seeded
1 cup mayonnaise
3 tablespoons chicken broth
3 tablespoons canned chipotle peppers
2 tablespoons soy sauce
2 tablespoons fresh lemon juice
2 tablespoons brown sugar
¹/₂ cup freshly grated Parmesan cheese

Soak the unhusked ears of corn in cold water for 1 hour; drain. Place the soaked ears directly on the oven rack. Roast at 400 degrees for 7 to 10 minutes or until tender, turning once. Remove the husks and silk when the corn is cool enough to handle.

Cut off enough kernels to measure 1 cup. Combine the corn kernels, lettuce and tomatoes in a large bowl. Whisk the mayonnaise, chicken broth, chipotle peppers, soy sauce, lemon juice and brown sugar in a bowl until well blended. Pour over the lettuce mixture. Add the Parmesan cheese; mix lightly. Divide the salad evenly among 4 plates. Garnish each serving with baby corn, tomato wedges and fresh Parmesan curls.

Serves Four

Tucson Medical Center
Todd Seligman,
Executive Chef 1991–1996

Calico Bean Salad

1 (14-ounce) can cut green beans,
  drained
1 (14-ounce) can wax beans, drained
1 (14-ounce) can kidney beans, drained
1 (14-ounce) can garbanzo beans,
  drained
1 cup white onion rings
$1/2$ cup chopped green bell pepper
2 ribs celery, chopped
$1/3$ cup vegetable oil
$2/3$ cup white vinegar
$1/2$ cup sugar
$1^1/2$ teaspoons salt
$1/4$ teaspoon garlic powder (optional)

Combine the green beans, wax beans,
kidney beans and garbanzo beans in a large
bowl. Add the onion, green pepper and
celery and mix lightly.

Whisk the oil, vinegar, sugar, salt and
garlic powder in a bowl until well blended.
Add to the bean mixture and toss lightly.

Refrigerate, covered, for 8 to 10 hours.
Stir just before serving.

Serves Twelve

Jalapeño Cole Slaw

8 pounds cabbage, shredded
2 large onions, chopped
8 fresh jalapeño peppers, finely chopped
2 cups olive oil
$3/4$ cup red wine vinegar
$1/4$ cup Dijon mustard
1 tablespoon mustard seeds
8 garlic cloves, minced
Salt and pepper to taste

Cook the cabbage in a large saucepan of
boiling water for 3 minutes; drain. Place in
a large bowl. Add the onions and peppers
and mix lightly.

Place the oil and vinegar in a blender
container. Process until well blended. Add
the mustard, mustard seeds, garlic, salt and
pepper. Process until well blended. Add to
the cabbage mixture and toss lightly.

Serves About Thirty-Six

Tanque Verde Guest Ranch
Mark Shelton, Executive Chef

Oriental Cabbage Salad

1/2 cup slivered almonds
2 tablespoons sesame seeds
1/2 head cabbage, shredded
3 to 4 green onions, chopped
3 tablespoons white vinegar
2 to 3 tablespoons vegetable oil
2 tablespoons sugar
1/4 teaspoon salt
1/4 teaspoon pepper
1 (3-ounce) package chicken-flavor
  ramen noodles

Place the almonds and sesame seeds in a shallow baking pan. Bake at 350 degrees for 8 to 10 minutes or until lightly toasted, stirring occasionally. Place in a large bowl. Add the cabbage and green onions and mix lightly.

Whisk the vinegar, oil, sugar, salt and pepper in a bowl. Stir in the contents of the seasoning packet from the ramen noodles.

Crumble the ramen noodles. Add the noodles and salad dressing to the cabbage mixture and toss lightly.

Serves Six to Eight

Curry Chicken Salad

1 (8-ounce) can pineapple chunks
1/2 cup reduced-calorie mayonnaise-type
    salad dressing
1 tablespoon Dijon mustard
1/2 teaspoon curry powder
4 cups chopped cooked chicken
2/3 cup golden raisins
2/3 cup slivered almonds, toasted
1/2 cup chopped celery

Drain the pineapple, reserving 3 tablespoons of the juice. Place the reserved juice in a large bowl.

Blend in the salad dressing, mustard and curry powder. Add the pineapple, chicken, raisins, almonds and celery and mix lightly.

Refrigerate, covered, for several hours or until chilled. Serve on a lettuce-lined platter if desired.

Serves Four to Six

Cold Chicken Sesame Salad

1/2 cup sesame oil
1 (3-pound) chicken, cooked, chopped
2 ounces sliced almonds
2 ounces sesame seeds
1/4 cup each white vinegar and sugar
2 teaspoons salt
1 teaspoon MSG
1/2 teaspoon pepper
1 head iceberg lettuce, shredded
4 to 6 green onions, sliced
6 radishes, thinly sliced
2 ounces rice noodles

Heat the oil in a large skillet over medium heat. Add the chicken. Cook until heated through, stirring occasionally. Remove the chicken from the skillet; drain and cool.

Lightly toast the almonds and sesame seeds in a shallow baking pan at 350 degrees for 10 minutes, stirring occasionally; cool.

Combine the vinegar, sugar, salt, MSG and pepper in a small saucepan. Cook over medium heat until the sugar is dissolved, stirring occasionally. Pour into a large bowl. Add the chicken, almonds and sesame seeds and toss lightly. Combine the lettuce, green onions, radishes and noodles in a bowl and mix lightly. Arrange the lettuce mixture on a serving platter. Top with the chicken mixture.

Serves Four to Six

Tucson Medical Center
Scott Schupmann, Chef 1983–1988

Buddy's Grill Chicken Salad

2 pounds chicken pieces, cooked
2 cups seedless grape halves
1½ cups toasted pecan pieces
1 bunch fresh chives, minced
Juice of ½ medium lemon
6 cups mayonnaise
3 cups plain yogurt
1 tablespoon celery salt

Cool the chicken; remove and discard the skin. Cut the chicken into bite-size pieces. Place in a large bowl. Add the grapes, pecans, chives and lemon juice and mix lightly.

Combine the mayonnaise, yogurt and celery salt in a bowl and mix well. Add 2 cups of the mayonnaise mixture to the chicken mixture and mix lightly. Reserve the remaining mayonnaise mixture for another use.

Serves Eight

Buddy's Grill

Chicken Salad with Grapes

1/3 cup white wine vinegar
2 tablespoons vegetable oil
1 tablespoon soy sauce
4 teaspoons sugar
1 teaspoon grated lemon peel
1/2 teaspoon dried thyme leaves, crushed
2 cups shredded cooked chicken
2 cups seedless green grapes, cut into
   halves
2 cups chicken broth
1 cup bulgur wheat
1/2 cup thin red bell pepper slices
1/2 cup diagonally sliced green onions
2 tablespoons chopped fresh parsley

Whisk the vinegar, oil, soy sauce, sugar, lemon peel and thyme in a bowl until well blended. Remove 1/2 cup of the vinegar mixture and divide it between 2 medium bowls.

Add the chicken to 1 bowl and the grapes to the other bowl, tossing to mix.

Bring the chicken broth to a boil in a medium saucepan. Stir in the bulgur.

Simmer, covered, over medium-low heat until the liquid is absorbed. Remove from the heat; cool.

Place the bulgur in a medium bowl. Add the red pepper, green onions and parsley and mix lightly. Spoon the bulgur mixture into a large shallow serving dish.

Drain the chicken and the grapes, reserving the vinegar mixture. Arrange the chicken and grapes in rows on top of the bulgur mixture. Refrigerate, covered, for 1 hour.

Combine both the reserved and remaining vinegar mixtures. Drizzle over the salad.

Serves Six

Grilled Chicken Salad

1 pound boneless skinless chicken breast
   halves, grilled
2 large tomatoes, chopped
1 medium zucchini, sliced
1 cup whole kernel corn
1 ripe avocado, peeled and sliced
1/3 cup sliced green onions
1/2 cup salsa or picante sauce
2 tablespoons vegetable oil
2 tablespoons chopped cilantro or
   fresh parsley
1 tablespoon lemon juice
1/2 teaspoon garlic salt
1/2 teaspoon cumin
Lettuce leaves

Cool the chicken; cut into bite-size pieces. Place in a large bowl. Add the tomatoes, zucchini, corn, avocado and green onions and mix lightly.

Combine the salsa, oil, cilantro, lemon juice, garlic salt and cumin in a bowl and mix well. Pour over the chicken mixture, mixing lightly.

Refrigerate, covered, for several hours or until chilled, stirring occasionally. Serve on lettuce-lined plates with additional salsa.

Serves Four

Salmon Salad

1 pound salmon fillet
Salt and pepper to taste
$^1/_3$ cup dry white wine
$^1/_3$ cup water
$^1/_4$ cup mayonnaise
Juice of $^1/_2$ medium lemon
1 medium onion, chopped
$^1/_3$ cup chopped center heart of celery
1 hard-cooked egg, finely grated
1 tablespoon chopped fresh parsley

Season the salmon lightly with salt and pepper. Place in a shallow baking dish. Add the wine and water. Bake at 350 degrees for 15 minutes or until the salmon is just cooked through and flakes easily.

Combine the mayonnaise and lemon juice in a large bowl. Add the onion, celery, egg and parsley and mix well.

Break the salmon into small pieces. Add to the mayonnaise mixture and mix lightly.

Refrigerate, covered, for 8 to 10 hours. Serve in phyllo cups with crackers or as a sandwich filling.

Note: May add the liquid from the baked salmon to the mixture, then mix with bread crumbs to make salmon patties. Dredge in additional bread crumbs and pan-fry or bake.

Serves Four to Six

Jonathan's Tucson Cork
Jonathan Landeen, Owner-Chef

Mexican Tuna Salad

$^1/_3$ cup sour cream
$^1/_2$ teaspoon ground cumin
$^1/_2$ teaspoon garlic salt
2 (6-ounce) cans tuna, drained
$^1/_2$ cup chopped seeded tomato
$^1/_4$ cup chopped green chiles
$^1/_4$ cup chopped celery
$^1/_4$ cup chopped green onions
Crisp salad greens
Tortilla chips

Combine the sour cream, cumin and garlic salt in a medium bowl. Add the tuna, tomato, chiles, celery and green onions and mix lightly.

Cover 4 salad plates with salad greens. Top with the tuna mixture. Serve with tortilla chips.

Serves Four

The Santa Catalina Mountains and Mount Lemmon

Tucson sits in a valley surrounded by mountains. The closest peaks are the ruggedly beautiful Santa Catalina Mountains. These mountains are a hiker's delight, with more than 150 miles of trails of varying degrees of difficulty. Mount Lemmon is the tallest of these peaks at 9,157 feet and can be easily reached via the Catalina Highway. This thirty-mile trip takes one through five distinct life zones, or areas that support specific types of vegetation. Starting at the bottom with the desert, one climbs through piñon and juniper forests, elevations supporting fir trees, and, at the top, aspen trees. Campgrounds are found along the way, as well as numerous pull-offs for scenic vistas.

At the top, Ski Valley is the southernmost ski area in the United States, when there is snow. Year-round, one can ride the ski lift to the very top of Mount Lemmon for a spectacular view. A restaurant provides the opportunity for a meal or refreshing drink. Starting down the mountain, a visit to the tiny village of Summerhaven is a must. With shops, restaurants, and overnight accommodations, the village also serves as the social and municipal support for those lucky enough to live on the mountain. Needless to say, Mount Lemmon is a frequent destination for those seeking to get away from Tucson's summer heat.

Tuna Salad Hawaiian

½ cup mayonnaise
1 tablespoon soy sauce
½ teaspoon salt
1 (20-ounce) can pineapple chunks,
*   drained*
2 (6-ounce) cans tuna, drained
½ cup chopped celery
½ cup sliced water chestnuts
¼ cup sliced green onions

Combine the mayonnaise, soy sauce and salt in a large bowl.

Add the pineapple, tuna, celery, water chestnuts and green onions and mix lightly.

Serves Four

Sirloin Citrus Salad

1 pound boneless beef top sirloin steak,
*   cut 1 inch thick, well trimmed*
1 teaspoon olive oil
Salt to taste
4 cups torn romaine lettuce
2 seedless oranges, peeled and separated
*   into sections*
2 tablespoons orange juice
2 tablespoons red wine vinegar
2 teaspoons olive oil
2 teaspoons honey
1¼ teaspoons Dijon mustard

Cut the steak into thin strips. Cut each strip crosswise into halves. Heat the oil in a large nonstick skillet over medium-high heat. Add half the steak. Stir-fry for 1 to 2 minutes or until evenly browned. Remove the steak from the skillet with a slotted spoon. Place in a large salad bowl and season with salt. Repeat with the remaining steak.

Add the lettuce and oranges to the steak and toss lightly. Whisk the orange juice, vinegar, oil, honey and mustard in a bowl. Drizzle over the salad. Garnish with strawberries.

Serves Four

Caesar Salad Dressing

2½ tablespoons chopped anchovies
2 egg yolks
1¼ tablespoons minced garlic
2 teaspoons lemon juice
1 teaspoon Dijon mustard
2 cups olive oil
⅓ cup grated Parmesan cheese
1¼ tablespoons lemon juice
2½ teaspoons Worcestershire sauce
2 teaspoons balsamic vinegar
1 teaspoon Tabasco sauce
Salt and pepper to taste

Place the anchovies, egg yolks, garlic, 2 teaspoons lemon juice and mustard in a blender container. Process until a smooth paste forms. Add the oil gradually with the blender running, processing until well blended. Add the Parmesan cheese, 1¼ tablespoons lemon juice, Worcestershire sauce, vinegar, Tabasco sauce, salt and pepper. Process until well blended. Serve on romaine hearts tossed with garlic croutons.

Serves Eight

Café Terra Cotta
Donna Nordin, Owner-Chef

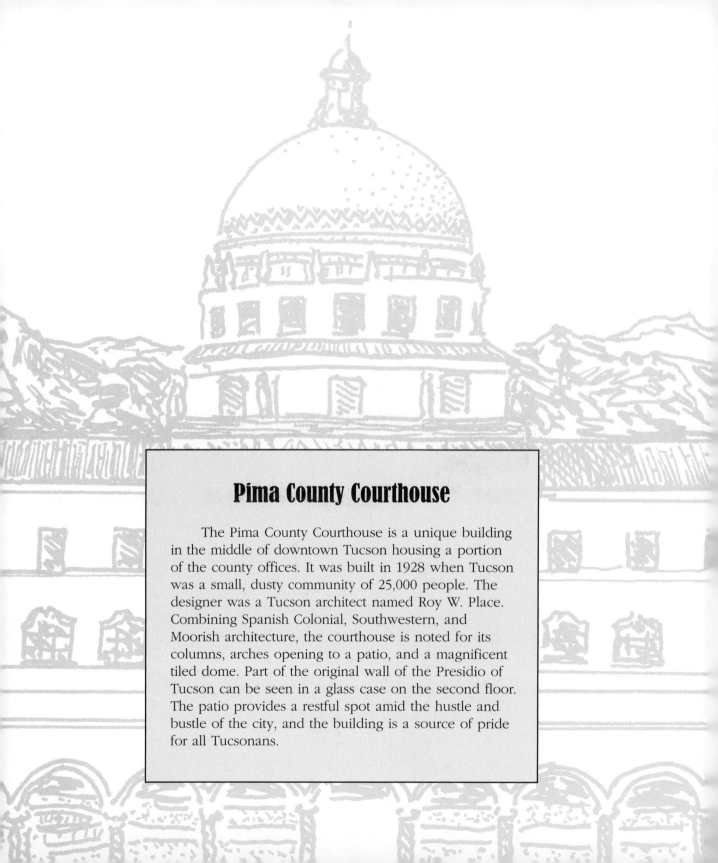

Pima County Courthouse

The Pima County Courthouse is a unique building in the middle of downtown Tucson housing a portion of the county offices. It was built in 1928 when Tucson was a small, dusty community of 25,000 people. The designer was a Tucson architect named Roy W. Place. Combining Spanish Colonial, Southwestern, and Moorish architecture, the courthouse is noted for its columns, arches opening to a patio, and a magnificent tiled dome. Part of the original wall of the Presidio of Tucson can be seen in a glass case on the second floor. The patio provides a restful spot amid the hustle and bustle of the city, and the building is a source of pride for all Tucsonans.

Entrées

Delicious Beef Roast

1 (3½- to 8-pound) beef eye of round
  roast
Salt and freshly ground black pepper
  to taste

Preheat the oven to 500 degrees or to the highest setting. Insert a meat thermometer in the roast so the tip of the thermometer is in the center of the thickest part of the roast. Season with salt and pepper.

Place on a rack in a shallow roasting pan. Bake for 4 to 5 minutes for each pound of beef. Turn off the oven and leave the oven door closed. Let the roast stand in the warm oven for 1½ to 2 hours or until the roast registers 140 degrees for rare or 160 degrees for medium.

The roast should be nicely browned on the outside and juicy inside. If the roast seems too cool when removed from the oven, reheat at 350 degrees to desired temperature.

Serves Six to Sixteen

Vegetable-Stuffed Baked Sirloin with Pepper Sauce

1 (9-ounce) top sirloin steak, butterflied
1/2 cup butter
1 red bell pepper, finely chopped
1 onion, finely chopped
5 mushrooms, chopped
2 slices pepper Jack cheese
1 sprig of fresh rosemary
1 medium onion, chopped
1/2 large carrot, chopped
1 rib celery, chopped
1 bay leaf
4 sprigs of fresh parsley
1 sprig of fresh thyme
2 teaspoons flour
3/4 cup dry red wine
1 tablespoon red wine vinegar
1/4 teaspoon pepper

Pound the steak to a 1/2-inch thickness; set aside. Melt 1/4 cup of the butter in a medium skillet. Add the red pepper, onion and mushrooms. Cook until tender, stirring occasionally. Place the cheese in the center of the steak. Top with the sautéed vegetables and rosemary. Fold the steak in half and wrap tightly in heavy-duty foil.

Bake at 350 degrees or until done to taste.

Melt the remaining 1/4 cup butter in a small saucepan over medium-high heat. Add the next 6 ingredients. Cook until the vegetables start to brown, stirring frequently. Reduce the heat to low. Add the flour all at once, stirring until the flour is browned.

Heat the wine and vinegar in a small saucepan until warm. Add to the vegetable mixture and mix until well blended. Bring to a boil over medium-high heat.

Reduce the heat to medium-low. Simmer, uncovered, for 20 minutes, stirring occasionally.

Unwrap the steak and place on a serving platter. Season the sauce with the pepper. Cook for 1 minute. Strain the sauce and spoon it over the steak.

Serves Two

Ye Olde Lantern
Kay Roberts, Chef

The Tucson Museum of Art

The Tucson Museum of Art is part of an historic block in downtown Tucson that also includes the Plaza of the Pioneers. The museum offers a varied year-round schedule of changing fine arts and crafts exhibits. Permanent collections include Western, pre-Columbian, Spanish Colonial, Twentieth Century European, and American art.

Near the museum is Casa Cordova, which is one of the oldest surviving buildings in Tucson.

The Junior League of Tucson has restored this house as a Mexican Heritage Museum with furnishings depicting the era in which it was built. This house includes a typical patio of the 1880s where residents cooked and frequently slept. The structure shows the ingenuity of the early settlers in using available building materials such as cactus, straw, and wood shavings. The museum house and patio stand in sharp contrast against the modern glass skyscrapers of Tucson today.

Spicy Pot Roast

2 tablespoons shortening
1 (3- to 5-pound) beef pot roast or
  chuck roast
1/2 cup packed brown sugar
1/2 cup vinegar
1/4 cup soy sauce
1/4 teaspoon salt
2 medium onions, cut into wedges
4 ribs celery, cut into 2-inch pieces
1 bay leaf
Flour

Melt the shortening in a Dutch oven over medium-high heat. Add the roast. Cook until the roast is evenly browned on all sides, turning occasionally.

Combine the brown sugar, vinegar, soy sauce and salt in a bowl and mix well. Pour over the roast. Add the onions, celery and bay leaf.

Simmer, covered, over medium-low heat for 2 hours or until the roast registers 160 degrees when a meat thermometer is inserted in the thickest part of the roast. Remove the roast from the pan, reserving the drippings in the pan. Discard the bay leaf.

Remove 1 cup of the drippings. Add 1 1/2 tablespoons flour to the removed drippings. Add an additional 1 1/2 tablespoons flour for each cup of meat drippings remaining in the pan. Stir the flour mixture until well blended. Add to the drippings remaining in the pan and mix well. Cook until the gravy is thickened, stirring constantly. Slice the roast and serve with the gravy and vegetables.

Note: May add carrots and/or peeled potatoes to the pan along with the onions and celery.

Serves Six to Eight

Sweet-and-Sour Brisket

1 (14-ounce) can stewed tomatoes
1 (8-ounce) can sauerkraut
1 cup applesauce
2 tablespoons brown sugar
1 (2½- to 3½-pound) beef brisket
2 tablespoons cornstarch
2 tablespoons cold water

Combine the undrained tomatoes, undrained sauerkraut, applesauce and brown sugar in a large skillet. Bring to a boil over medium-high heat. Add the brisket, spooning the tomato mixture over the top.

Reduce the heat to medium-low. Simmer, covered, for 2½ to 3 hours or until the brisket is tender, occasionally spooning the tomato mixture over the brisket. Transfer the brisket to a serving platter, reserving the drippings in the pan. Cover the brisket to keep it warm. Skim the excess fat from the drippings and discard.

Combine the cornstarch and water in a bowl, mixing until blended. Stir into the drippings in the skillet. Cook over medium-high heat until the gravy comes to a boil and thickens, stirring frequently. Cook for an additional 2 minutes.

Slice the brisket across the grain into ¼-inch-thick slices and place on a serving platter. Spoon some of the gravy over the brisket; serve the remainder on the side. Garnish with fresh parsley sprigs.

Serves Six to Eight

Grilled Tenderloin with Pepper Sauce

Cracked black pepper
1 (2-pound) beef tenderloin
Salt
1 cup pinot noir
1 tablespoon red pepper vodka
4 garlic cloves, crushed
4 sprigs of fresh rosemary
2 bay leaves
1 cup chicken broth
1 tablespoon tomato paste

Press the black pepper into the surface of the tenderloin; sprinkle with salt. Place in a large roasting pan.

Combine the wine, vodka, garlic, rosemary and bay leaves in a bowl. Pour over the tenderloin. Marinate in the refrigerator for 20 minutes, turning occasionally.

Remove the tenderloin from the marinade; reserve the marinade. Grill over hot coals for 10 minutes per side or until a meat thermometer registers 135 degrees for medium-rare. (For medium doneness, grill to an internal temperature of 150 degrees.) Let stand for 15 minutes before carving into 3/4-inch-thick slices.

Pour the reserved marinade into a saucepan. Stir in the broth and tomato paste. Bring to a boil. Simmer until reduced by half, stirring occasionally.

Remove and discard the bay leaves. Serve the tenderloin with mashed potatoes and vegetables topped with the sauce.

Serve Six

95

Tournedos of Beef with Artichokes and Mushrooms

1 (10-ounce) beef tenderloin, cut into
    4 equal pieces
1 tablespoon butter
4 canned artichoke hearts, cut into
    halves
1/2 cup mushroom halves
1 tablespoon minced fresh garlic
1 tablespoon chopped shallots
1 cup brown sauce
1 cup burgundy
1/2 cup béarnaise sauce

Heat a large skillet over high heat. Add the tenderloin pieces. Cook until browned on both sides. Remove the tenderloins from the skillet and place in a shallow baking pan. Bake, covered, at 350 degrees for 5 minutes or until done to taste.

Melt the butter in the same skillet over medium-high heat. Add the artichokes, mushrooms, garlic and shallots. Cook until the mushrooms are tender, stirring occasionally. Stir in the brown sauce and wine. Reduce the heat to medium-low. Simmer until the sauce is slightly thickened, stirring occasionally.

Place the tenderloins on a serving platter. Top with the artichoke sauce and the béarnaise sauce.

Serves Two

Charles Restaurant
Joeseph Dessault, Executive Chef

Fillets with Tarragon Butter

4 teaspoons butter, softened
2 tablespoons finely minced shallots
    (about 2 whole)
1 teaspoon tarragon
1 teaspoon olive oil
2 fillets of beef, 2 inches thick (about
    3/4 pound)
Salt and pepper to taste

Melt 1 teaspoon of the butter in a small skillet. Add the shallots. Cook for 3 to 4 minutes or until the shallots begin to brown, stirring occasionally. Remove from the heat. Stir in the remaining 3 teaspoons butter and the tarragon; let cool.

Divide the butter mixture into 2 mounds and flatten each mound between 2 sheets of waxed paper. Freeze until ready to use.

Heat the oil in a large ovenproof skillet or baking pan over high heat. Season the fillets with salt and pepper. Add the fillets to the skillet. Cook until evenly browned on both sides.

Remove the skillet from the heat and place it in a 400-degree oven. Bake for 5 minutes for medium-rare. Remove the fillets from the oven and let stand for several minutes before serving. Serve each fillet topped with a portion of the tarragon butter.

Serves Two

The Wishing Shrine

This small shrine is located in downtown Tucson just south of the Civic Center in a neighborhood called The Barrio. It has been preserved as a monument, but the legends vary as to what or who is being honored.

All the legends seem to include a love triangle in which someone dies and is buried at this spot. Residents light candles for this person and for the souls of others, and the belief is that if the candle stays lit all night, the prayer will be answered.

The shrine has been listed in the National Register of Historic Places and, due to this, the neighborhood was recently spared from destruction by a federally funded freeway planned for the area. This was a decisive win for the proponents of historic preservation.

Sliced Tenderloin of Beef

1 (4- to 5-pound) trimmed beef
    tenderloin
3 tablespoons butter
1 pound mushrooms, sliced
1 tablespoon vegetable oil
3/4 cup beef stock
3/4 cup burgundy
2 tablespoons cornstarch
1/3 cup beef stock

The day before serving, place the tenderloin in a roasting pan. Roast at 450 degrees for 10 minutes. Reduce the heat to 350 degrees. Roast for 10 minutes for each pound of tenderloin. Remove from the oven. Refrigerate, covered, until ready to use.

Early the next day, melt 1 tablespoon of the butter in a large skillet over medium-high heat. Add the mushrooms. Cook until tender, stirring occasionally.

Remove the mushrooms from the skillet. Add the remaining 2 tablespoons butter and oil. Heat until the butter is melted. Stir in 3/4 cup beef stock and the wine.

Blend the cornstarch with 1/3 cup beef stock in a bowl and add to the skillet. Cook until the sauce is thickened, stirring frequently. Stir in the mushrooms. Remove from the heat. Slice the tenderloin and rearrange in its original shape (as if it had not been sliced) in a 9x13-inch baking dish. Top with the sauce. Cover and refrigerate.

About 1 hour before baking, remove the tenderloin from the refrigerator and let stand at room temperature. Bake at 275 degrees for 1 hour or until heated through. Serve with cooked wild rice, lemon-glazed carrots and a tossed salad.

Serves Twelve to Fifteen

Boeuf Bourguignonne

6 slices bacon, cut into ¹/₂-inch pieces
1 (3-pound) beef rump or chuck roast,
    cut into 1¹/₂-inch cubes
1 large carrot, peeled and sliced
1 medium onion, sliced
3 tablespoons flour
1¹/₂ teaspoons salt
¹/₈ teaspoon pepper
1 (10-ounce) can beef broth
1¹/₂ cups burgundy or other dry
    red wine
1 tablespoon tomato paste or catsup
2 garlic cloves, minced
¹/₂ pound pearl onions, peeled
¹/₂ to 1 teaspoon minced fresh thyme
1 bay leaf
1 pound mushrooms, sliced
4 tablespoons butter, softened
¹/₄ cup flour

Cook the bacon in a large skillet over medium heat until crisp, stirring occasionally. Remove the bacon from the skillet and drain the fat. Add the beef to the skillet. Cook until evenly browned, stirring occasionally. Remove from the skillet, reserving the drippings in the skillet.

Place the beef in a slow cooker. Add the carrot and sliced onion to the skillet. Cook for 5 minutes or until browned, stirring occasionally. Add 3 tablespoons flour, salt and pepper and mix well. Stir in the broth, wine, tomato paste and garlic. Add to the slow cooker. Add the bacon, pearl onions, thyme and bay leaf.

Cook, covered, on Low for 8 to 10 hours. Sauté the mushrooms in 2 tablespoons of the butter until tender. Add to the slow cooker. Cook, covered, for 1 hour.

Combine the remaining 2 tablespoons butter and ¹/₄ cup flour in a bowl and mix until blended. Roll into small balls. Add to the ingredients in the slow cooker and cover. Increase the heat to High and bring the sauce to a boil. Simmer until thickened. Discard the bay leaf. Serve the beef mixture over hot buttered noodles.

Note: May substitute canned or frozen pearl onions for the fresh pearl onions.

Serves Twelve

Beef Stew

2 tablespoons flour
2 tablespoons soy sauce
2 pounds stew beef, cut into chunks
4 carrots, cut into chunks
2 large onions, sliced
1 cup thinly sliced celery
1 cup red wine or beef consommé
$^1/_4$ teaspoon pepper
$^1/_4$ teaspoon marjoram
$^1/_4$ teaspoon thyme
1 cup sliced mushrooms

Combine the flour and soy sauce in a 2$^1/_2$- to 3-quart baking dish. Add the stew beef and toss to coat. Add the carrots, onions, celery, wine, pepper, marjoram and thyme and mix well.

Bake, tightly covered, at 325 degrees for 1 hour. Stir in the mushrooms.

Bake, covered, for 1$^1/_2$ to 2 hours or until the beef and vegetables are tender. Serve over rice or noodles.

Serves Six to Eight

Magnificent Meatloaf

2 eggs, beaten
1/2 cup sour cream
1/2 cup catsup
1 1/4 cups fine bread crumbs
4 large carrots, finely shredded
1 (4-ounce) can sliced mushrooms,
    drained (optional)
1 rib celery with leaves, finely chopped
1 1/2 tablespoons finely chopped onion
2 tablespoons grated Parmesan cheese
1/2 teaspoon garlic salt
1/4 teaspoon thyme
1/4 teaspoon pepper
2 pounds ground sirloin

Combine the eggs, sour cream and catsup in a large bowl. Add the bread crumbs, carrots, mushrooms, celery, onion, Parmesan cheese, garlic salt, thyme and pepper. Mix until well blended. Add the ground sirloin and mix lightly.

Shape into a loaf in a shallow baking dish or press into a 5x9-inch baking pan. Bake at 350 degrees for 1 1/4 to 1 1/2 hours or until cooked through. Remove from the oven. Let stand for 5 minutes before slicing to serve.

Note: May process the bread slices in a food processor or blender container to get the measured amount of crumbs. Place the carrots and celery in the food processor or blender container to shred and chop.

Serves Eight

Old Tucson Studios

Old Tucson Studios, located twelve miles west of Tucson, was originally built as a set for the movie Arizona *in 1939. It recreates the Tucson of the 1860s with adobe or frontier buildings, board sidewalks, and dusty streets. More than 250 movies have been filmed there, along with numerous television shows and commercials.*

A popular tourist destination, the park provides stunt shows, staged shootouts, magic shows, and musical revues in the saloon. In addition, there are train and stagecoach rides and a small amusement park area. Many shops and food venues make this a fun day for the whole family.

Old Tucson, virtually destroyed by a fire in 1995, reopened in 1997, bigger and better than ever.

The daily crowds attest to the fact that the Old West and cowboys continue to have endless appeal for many people.

Quick-and-Easy Meat and Potato Pie

4 large potatoes
Milk
Butter
1 pound ground beef
1 (12-ounce) jar beef-flavor gravy
1 (1-ounce) package dry onion
  soup mix
6 medium carrots, chopped and cooked
Paprika

Peel the potatoes and cut into bite-size pieces. Add to a large saucepan of boiling water. Cook until tender; drain. Return the potatoes to the saucepan and mash, adding desired amounts of milk and butter.

Brown the ground beef in a skillet, stirring until crumbly; drain. Add the gravy, soup mix and carrots and mix well. Spoon into a 6x10-inch baking dish. Top with the mashed potatoes, spreading the potatoes to completely cover the ground beef mixture.

Score decorative lines in the potatoes with a fork if desired. Sprinkle lightly with paprika. Bake at 375 degrees for 30 minutes or until the potatoes are golden brown.

Serves Four

Hearty Beef and Cheese Pie

1¹/₄ pounds ground beef
¹/₃ cup chopped onion
¹/₄ cup chopped green bell pepper
1 (8-ounce) can tomato sauce
¹/₄ teaspoon garlic salt
1 (8-count) can crescent rolls
1 egg, lightly beaten
2 cups shredded Monterey Jack cheese

Brown the ground beef with the onion and green pepper in a large skillet, stirring until the ground beef is crumbly; drain. Stir in the tomato sauce and garlic salt.

Unroll the crescent dough on a nonstick surface and separate it into triangles. Arrange the triangles in an ungreased 9-inch pie plate, placing the points of the triangles in the center and the wide ends up the side of the dish. Press the edges of the triangles together to seal.

Combine the egg and 1 cup of the cheese in a bowl and mix well. Spread over the pastry shell. Top with the ground beef mixture. Sprinkle with the remaining 1 cup cheese.

Bake at 375 degrees for 20 to 25 minutes or until the crust is golden brown.

Serves Six

Hamburger Pie with Scones

1 pound ground beef
¹/₄ cup flour
1 teaspoon salt
¹/₄ teaspoon pepper
2 cups tomato juice or vegetable juice cocktail
1 cup chopped celery
¹/₂ cup chopped onion
¹/₄ cup chopped green bell pepper
1¹/₂ cups flour
2 teaspoons baking powder
1 teaspoon salt
1 egg
¹/₃ cup vegetable oil
¹/₃ cup milk

Brown the ground beef in a large skillet, stirring until crumbly; drain. Add the ¹/₄ cup flour, 1 teaspoon salt and pepper and mix well. Stir in the tomato juice, celery, onion and green pepper.

Bring to a boil; simmer over medium-low heat for 10 minutes. Spoon into a greased 1¹/₂-quart baking dish.

Sift the 1¹/₂ cups flour, baking powder and 1 teaspoon salt into a medium bowl.

Whisk the egg, oil and milk in a bowl until well blended. Add to the flour mixture and stir just until the dry ingredients are moistened. Drop the dough by mounded tablespoonfuls over the ground beef mixture.

Bake at 425 degrees for 30 to 35 minutes or until the topping is golden brown.

Serves Four or Five

Tucson Medical Center Gift Shop

The Tucson Medical Center Gift Shop, the chief fund-raising arm of the Auxiliary, had humble beginnings. Volunteers sold combs and toothbrushes from a drawer at the information desk in the main lobby. With the official founding of the Auxiliary in 1949, it was felt that there should be a year-round fund-raising project that would swell the coffers of the Auxiliary and be of service to the hospital.

Mrs. Esther Levy, whose husband owned a local department store, presented the idea of a display case, stocked with items bought at cost from Levy's store. Sundries and small gift items were also taken on a wicker cart to patients' rooms. A "good week" brought in ten dollars in sales. Soon a second case was added and business improved.

By 1960, a larger Gift Shop space was made available in a corridor off the main lobby, and soon the Gift Shop could boast of over four hundred items available for sale.

In 1962, the Gift Shop moved out of the hall into the remodeled business office space. Inventory expanded, volunteer buyers attended gift shows to procure the latest merchandise, and volunteer salesladies received training from local department store personnel. Display cases were located in the various lobbies around the hospital. Adopting the motto "Remember that a Gift Shop gift gives twice," the retail outlet was making an important

contribution to the Auxiliary's annual gift to TMC.

In 1967, the Gift Shop was expanded in size, and buyers were appointed for each department in the shop. The first style show, with clothing and accessories from the Gift Shop modeled by Auxilians, was presented in 1968. Three or four hall sales a year appeased the bargain hunters and created space for new merchandise. In addition, the Gift Shop participated in the annual Christmas Bazaar staged by the ladies of the Auxiliary Craft Shop.

A move to its present location was made in 1980. With wood fixtures and still newer lines of merchandise, the Gift Shop was a most popular destination for visitors and employees. By 1988, a cosmetic renovation was necessary and accomplished. With the reopening, the Gift Shop accepted credit cards for the first time. A payroll deduction program was established for employee shoppers and this proved most beneficial for the Gift Shop and the employees. Sales improved dramatically and employees enjoyed having an interest-free charge account.

By 1990, running the Gift Shop seven days a week had become a huge responsibility for volunteers, and it was decided to hire full-time professional management. The shop would continue, however, to be staffed by volunteer sales personnel.

In 1995, the Gift Shop was closed for a major remodeling. The reopening in March 1995 was accompanied by much-deserved fanfare. The shop was half again as large, with abundant windows and natural lighting showcasing the soft desert colors and the many new merchandise lines.

The success of today's Gift Shop rests squarely on the shoulders of savvy management ably assisted by paid personnel in the evenings and on weekends. Our very capable volunteers continue to provide staffing weekdays. The Gift Shop stocks apparel, gift items, jewelry and other accessory items, toys, fresh flowers, sundries, and lots of chocolate. It is a most popular place with employees, who make up 85 percent of the customer base. Visitors are amazed at the variety of items available and frequently return to shop after their loved ones are dismissed.

Remember when a "good" week's profit was ten dollars? This year, the Gift Shop was proud to give the Auxiliary and Tucson Medical Center $300,000.

Beef Enchiladas

2 cups chopped cooked beef or pork
2 small onions, finely chopped
1 cup pitted black olives, chopped
1 teaspoon salt
1 tablespoon vegetable oil
3 (8-ounce) cans tomato sauce
1 (4-ounce) can chopped green chiles
1 tablespoon chili powder
12 tortillas
1 cup shredded Monterey Jack cheese
Chopped green onions

Combine the beef, half the chopped onions, olives and salt in a bowl and mix well. Heat the oil in a large skillet over medium-high heat. Add the remaining chopped onions. Cook until tender but not brown, stirring occasionally.

Stir in the tomato sauce, undrained chiles and chili powder. Simmer over medium-low heat for 10 minutes, stirring occasionally. Dip the tortillas 1 at a time into the tomato sauce mixture to soften. Place on a large plate.

Spoon about $1/4$ cup of the beef mixture down the center of each tortilla and roll up. Place seam side down in an 8x12-inch baking dish. Cover with the remaining tomato sauce mixture. Sprinkle with the cheese.

Bake at 350 degrees for 15 minutes or until heated through. Top with the green onions.

Note: Serve topped with additional chopped green chiles, onion and shredded cheese if desired. For a milder flavor, decrease the amount of chili powder used to 1 or 2 teaspoons.

Serves Four to Six

Layered Enchilada Pie

1 pound ground beef
1 medium onion, chopped
1 (8-ounce) can tomato sauce
1 tablespoon chili powder
1 teaspoon oregano
1 teaspoon salt
1/4 teaspoon pepper
1/4 teaspoon garlic salt
6 corn tortillas, buttered
1 (5-ounce) jar green olives, drained
    and chopped
1 1/2 cups shredded sharp Cheddar cheese
1 cup water

Brown the ground beef with the onion in a large skillet, stirring until the ground beef is crumbly; drain. Stir in the tomato sauce, chili powder, oregano, salt, pepper and garlic salt.

Layer the tortillas, ground beef sauce, olives and cheese 1/2 at a time in a greased round 2-quart baking dish. Pour the water into the baking dish.

Bake, covered, at 400 degrees for 20 minutes or until heated through. Cut into wedges to serve.

Serves Six

Leftover Taco Casserole

2 pounds ground beef
1 medium onion, chopped
2 (14-ounce) cans stewed tomatoes,
    crushed
2 (16-ounce) cans pinto beans, drained
2 cups cooked Spanish rice
3 cups shredded Cheddar cheese
Leftover taco shells, broken into pieces

Brown the ground beef in a large skillet, stirring until crumbly; drain. Add the onion. Simmer for 15 minutes or until the onion is tender, stirring occasionally.

Layer the ground beef mixture, undrained tomatoes, beans, rice and cheese in a 9x13-inch baking dish.

Bake at 325 degrees for 20 minutes or until the mixture is heated through and the cheese is melted. Serve with the taco shell pieces.

Note: Reheat the rice before layering in the baking dish for best results.

Serves Eight

Uniforms

When the Tucson Medical Center Auxiliary was formed in 1949, the first order of business was to join The National Hospital Association of Auxilians. In accordance with the national organization's standards, a uniform consisting of a cherry pink jumper with a white blouse was adopted. Over the years, styles have changed with jackets, aprons, and polo shirts added to the approved list of apparel—but always in cherry pink.

A Junior Auxiliary was formed in 1957 and these teenage girls wore red and white striped jumpers with white blouses and soon were called "candy stripers." In the 1980s, teenage boys requested membership, and the uniform changed to red polo shirts and white slacks or shorts.

Men joined the ranks in 1969, and a gold jacket with the Auxiliary logo on the pocket was adopted. Later, a lightweight blue jacket was made the official uniform for male Auxilians, with a collared polo shirt in white or peach offered as a warm weather alternative.

With uniforms offered in several styles in a rich shade of teal blue, 1999 finds a new look for the Auxiliary. Going into a new millennium, it seems appropriate to enter with an updated look and color.

Mexican Lasagna

1¹/₂ pounds ground beef
1 medium onion, chopped
1 (2¹/₄-ounce) can pitted black olives
1 (14-ounce) can diced tomatoes
1 (10-ounce) can enchilada sauce
1 teaspoon salt
¹/₄ teaspoon garlic powder
¹/₈ teaspoon pepper
¹/₄ cup vegetable oil
8 corn tortillas
1 egg, beaten
1 cup small curd cottage cheese
2 cups shredded Monterey Jack cheese
¹/₂ cup shredded Cheddar cheese
¹/₂ cup finely crushed tortilla chips

Brown the ground beef with the onion in a large skillet, stirring until the ground beef is crumbly; drain. Drain the olives, reserving the liquid.

Chop the olives. Add the olives and reserved liquid to the skillet. Stir in the undrained tomatoes, enchilada sauce, salt, garlic powder and pepper. Bring the mixture to a boil.

Simmer, uncovered, over medium-low heat for 20 minutes, stirring occasionally.

Heat the oil in a small skillet over medium heat. Dip the tortillas 1 at a time into the hot oil to soften. Drain the tortillas and cut into halves.

Combine the egg and cottage cheese in a bowl and mix well. Spread ¹/₃ of the ground beef mixture over the bottom of a greased round 3-quart baking dish.

Top with half the Monterey Jack cheese, half the cottage cheese mixture and half the tortillas. Repeat the layers. Top with the remaining ground beef mixture and Cheddar cheese. Sprinkle the chips around the outer edge of the baking dish.

Bake at 350 degrees for 30 minutes or until heated through.

Serves Twelve

Southwestern Veal Chops with Tomato Green Chile Sauce

4 veal chops, trimmed
Salt and pepper to taste
Paprika
2 cups chopped fresh tomatoes
2 cups tomato sauce
1 poblano chile, roasted, skinned and
   seeded
Chili powder
Cumin
Minced fresh garlic

Season the veal with salt, pepper and paprika. Heat a large skillet over medium-high heat. Add the veal. Cook until browned on both sides. Place in a shallow baking dish.

Bake at 400 degrees for 10 to 15 minutes or until no longer pink in the center.

Combine the tomatoes and tomato sauce in a medium saucepan. Simmer over medium heat until reduced by half, stirring occasionally. Chop the chile. Add to the saucepan and mix well. Simmer for 10 minutes. Season with chili powder, cumin, garlic, salt and pepper.

Place the veal on a serving platter. Top with the sauce.

Serves Four

Tanque Verde Guest Ranch
Mark Shelton, Executive Chef

Braised Lamb Shanks

2 tablespoons vegetable oil
4 lamb shanks
2 carrots, sliced
1 onion, sliced
2 ribs celery, chopped
1 garlic clove, minced
1 (14-ounce) can diced tomatoes
1 cup dry red wine
1 teaspoon salt
1/3 teaspoon pepper
1/3 teaspoon thyme
1/3 teaspoon parsley flakes

Heat the oil in a Dutch oven over medium-high heat. Add the lamb. Cook until browned on both sides.

Add the carrots, onion, celery and garlic. Cook over low heat until the vegetables are tender and golden brown, stirring occasionally. Stir in the undrained tomatoes, wine, salt, pepper, thyme and parsley flakes.

Bring to a boil; reduce the heat to low. Simmer, covered, for 2 hours or until the lamb is cooked through.

Serves Four

Tucson Medical Center Auxiliary Love Light Tree

The Love Light Tree, a fund-raiser, was first sponsored by the Tucson Medical Center Auxiliary in 1990. Donors bought white lights in memory of loved ones, and green or red lights to honor family, friends, and co-workers. A very large Christmas tree was set up outside the south entrance of the hospital and strung with red, green, and white lights. On a cool evening three weeks before Christmas, a short program was held to dedicate the tree and the lights were turned on. It was truly beautiful. A reception afterwards warmed up attendees and a tradition was born.

In 1992, it was decided to use the proceeds from Love Light sales to provide extra comforts to Hospice patients. When the Hospice Program moved to the Erickson Residence on the TMC campus, it seemed only fitting to decorate the large living tree outside that building as the Love Light Tree. It is always awesome and very touching when the switch is activated and all the lights shine in the darkness. One is compelled to stop and think of the lives represented there.

Tucson Medical Center Hospice Program

Hospice is a special program that cares for people with any terminal illness after the physician, the patient, and the family decide that aggressive treatment is no longer appropriate. Hospice affirms life and regards dying as a normal process. The Hospice Team, consisting of a Medical Director who oversees the program, a Hospice Manager, nursing personnel, social workers, and numerous volunteers, provides care and support as needed to the patient and the family. These dedicated and caring people are available around the clock, which is a great source of comfort to all involved.

The Hospice Program at TMC was begun in 1992 after several years of planning. Eight beds on Unit 600 were designated as Hospice beds, with extra comforts added to make the rooms more home-like. Still, 85 percent of Hospice patients prefer to remain at home for their care.

In 1997, Hospice realized its goal to have quarters of its own when the Papago Building was made available. A chapel, dining room, family room, and six patient rooms were opened and dedicated. Today, twelve patient rooms are available for those patients requiring more care than can be managed in the home. Families are very appreciative of the attention and support given by this very special service.

Perfect Pork Tenderloin

$1/4$ cup soy sauce
$1/4$ cup bourbon
2 tablespoons brown sugar
1 (1-pound) pork tenderloin
$1/3$ cup sour cream
1 tablespoon dry mustard
$1/3$ cup mayonnaise
1 tablespoon chopped green onions
1 teaspoon vinegar
Salt to taste

Combine the soy sauce, bourbon and brown sugar in a bowl. Mix until well blended. Place the tenderloin in a shallow baking pan. Pour the soy sauce mixture over the tenderloin.

Refrigerate, covered, for 1 hour, occasionally spooning the soy sauce mixture over the tenderloin. Remove the tenderloin from the refrigerator.

Bake, uncovered, at 325 degrees for 1 hour or until the tenderloin registers 160 degrees on a meat thermometer, basting occasionally with the soy sauce mixture.

Combine the sour cream, dry mustard, mayonnaise, green onions, vinegar and salt in a bowl and mix until blended. Serve with the tenderloin.

Serves Three or Four

Cranberry Pork Roast

1 ($2^1/2$- to 3-pound) boneless pork loin roast
1 (16-ounce) can jellied cranberry sauce
$1/2$ cup sugar
$1/2$ cup cranberry juice
1 teaspoon dry mustard
$1/4$ teaspoon cinnamon
$1/4$ teaspoon cloves
2 tablespoons cornstarch
2 tablespoons cold water
Salt to taste

Place the pork roast in a slow cooker. Mash the cranberry sauce in a medium bowl with a fork. Stir in the sugar, cranberry juice, dry mustard, cinnamon and cloves. Pour over the roast.

Cook, covered, on Low for 6 to 8 hours or until the roast is cooked through. Remove the roast from the slow cooker. Cover it to keep warm.

Skim the fat from the juices in the slow cooker. Pour the juices into a measuring cup. Add enough water to measure 2 cups. Pour into a medium saucepan. Bring to a boil over medium-high heat.

Combine the cornstarch and cold water in a bowl. Add to the saucepan. Cook until thickened, stirring constantly. Season with salt. Slice the roast and serve with the sauce.

Serves Six

Stuffed Pork Chops

6 to 8 pork chops, 1 1/2 inches thick
1 cup shredded Cheddar cheese
1/2 cup cooked rice
1/4 cup chopped pecans
1/4 cup chopped green bell pepper
1/4 cup chopped celery
1/2 teaspoon thyme
2 tablespoons vegetable oil
1 teaspoon salt
1/4 teaspoon pepper

Cut a slit in the side of each pork chop forming a pocket. Combine the cheese, rice, pecans, green pepper, celery and thyme in a bowl. Spoon about 1/4 cup of the rice mixture into the pocket in each of the pork chops.

Heat the oil in a large skillet. Add the stuffed chops. Cook until browned on both sides. Place the chops on a rack in a roasting pan. Season with the salt and pepper. Cover the pan with foil.

Bake at 350 degrees for 30 minutes. Bake, uncovered, for 30 minutes longer or until the pork chops are cooked through.

Note: The pockets in the pork chops will close during the cooking to seal in the stuffing. No skewers are needed.

Serves Six to Eight

Baked Pork Chop Casserole with Mushroom Sauce

3/4 cup flour
1 teaspoon salt
1/2 teaspoon pepper
6 pork chops, 3/4 to 1 inch thick
2 tablespoons vegetable oil
1 (10-ounce) can cream of mushroom
*   soup*
1 cup sour cream
2/3 cup chicken broth
1/2 teaspoon ginger
1/4 teaspoon rosemary
1 (2-ounce) can French-fried onions

Combine the flour, salt and pepper in a
shallow bowl. Add the pork chops 1 at a
time, turning to coat both sides with the
flour mixture.

Heat the oil in a large skillet. Add the
pork chops. Cook for 5 minutes on each
side or until browned. Place the pork chops
in a single layer in an ungreased 9x13-inch
baking dish.

Combine the soup and 1/2 cup of the
sour cream in a medium bowl. Stir in the
broth, ginger and rosemary. Pour over the
pork chops. Sprinkle with half the onions.

Bake, covered, at 350 degrees for
50 minutes. Stir the remaining 1/2 cup sour
cream into the sauce in the baking dish.
Sprinkle the remaining onions over the pork
chops. Bake, uncovered, for 10 minutes.

Serves Six

No-Fuss Pork Chops

6 pork chops, 3/4 to 1 inch thick
1 cup applesauce
1/4 cup soy sauce
1/8 teaspoon onion powder

Cook the pork chops in a nonstick skillet
coated with nonstick cooking spray over
medium-high heat until browned on both
sides. Place in a single layer in a shallow
baking pan.

Combine the applesauce, soy sauce and
onion powder in a bowl. Spoon evenly over
the pork chops. Cover the pan with foil.

Bake at 350 degrees for 45 minutes;
uncover. Bake for 15 minutes or until the
pork chops are tender and cooked through.

Note: For easy cleanup, line the baking pan
with foil. Potatoes may be baked in the
pan around the pork chops.

Serves Six

Men in the Auxiliary

Like most auxiliaries, the volunteer organization at Tucson Medical Center was initially a "ladies" group. In 1969, men were admitted to the ranks of TMC Auxiliary. Gold blazers were selected as attire for these few lonely souls.

Today, we are blessed with a large male membership. Fall always sees an influx of college-age volunteers, but the basic male membership is made up of retired gentlemen. These stalwarts bring to the organization their knowledge, experience, and abilities. We have retired military personnel, postmen, architects, doctors, lawyers, farmers, factory workers, and businessmen of every description. The hospital could not afford to hire these men, but they cheerfully give of their time. A new millennium will find them attired in the new teal blazer or a white shirt with the Auxiliary logo. Regardless of what they wear, we couldn't get along without them. History was made in 1998 with the election of the first male president of the Auxiliary. It is doubtful that he will be the last.

Quick Sweet-and-Sour Pork

2 tablespoons corn oil
1 pound boneless pork, cut into
    1-inch cubes
1 (15-ounce) can pineapple chunks
1/2 cup dark corn syrup
1/4 cup vinegar
2 tablespoons catsup
2 tablespoons soy sauce
1 garlic clove, minced
2 tablespoons cornstarch
2 tablespoons water
1/2 cup chopped green bell pepper
Hot cooked rice

Heat the oil in a large skillet over medium-high heat. Add the pork cubes. Cook until evenly browned on all sides, stirring frequently.

Add the undrained pineapple, corn syrup, vinegar, catsup, soy sauce and garlic and mix well.

Bring to a boil; reduce the heat to medium-low. Simmer for 10 minutes or until the pork is cooked through.

Combine the cornstarch and water in a bowl and mix until well blended. Stir into the pork mixture. Add the green pepper. Simmer for 2 minutes, stirring constantly. Serve over the rice.

Serves Four

Party Ham Casserole

1 (10-ounce) package frozen chopped
    broccoli
12 bread slices
3 cups shredded Cheddar cheese
2 cups chopped cooked ham
6 eggs, lightly beaten
3 1/2 cups milk
2 tablespoons minced onions
1/2 teaspoon salt
1/4 teaspoon dry mustard

Cook the broccoli according to the package directions; drain. Cut a circle from each of the bread slices with a round biscuit or cookie cutter.

Place the bread trimmings in a buttered 9x13-inch baking dish. Sprinkle with the cheese. Cover with the broccoli and ham. Top with the bread cutouts.

Whisk the eggs, milk, onions, salt and dry mustard in a bowl until well blended. Pour over the bread. Refrigerate, covered, for 8 to 10 hours.

Bake, uncovered, at 325 degrees for 25 minutes. Sprinkle with additional cheese if desired. Let stand for 10 minutes before cutting into squares to serve.

Note: May trim the crusts from the bread slices before using.

Serves Twelve

Cauliflower and Ham Bake

1 small head cauliflower
1 (10-ounce) can cream of celery soup
¹/₂ cup milk
¹/₂ teaspoon salt
¹/₈ teaspoon pepper
1 to 1¹/₂ cups chopped cooked ham
¹/₂ cup minced green onions
¹/₂ cup bread crumbs
Butter or margarine

Separate the cauliflower into florets. Cook in a small amount of boiling water in a saucepan for 8 to 10 minutes or until tender-crisp; drain.

Combine the soup, milk, salt and pepper in a bowl. Alternate layers of cauliflower, ham, green onions and soup mixture in a buttered 2-quart baking dish until all ingredients are used. Top with the bread crumbs. Dot with desired amount of butter.

Bake at 375 degrees for 20 to 30 minutes or until the bread crumbs are browned.

Serves Four to Six

Ham Balls on Pineapple

2¹/₂ cups ground cooked ham
¹/₂ cup rolled oats
¹/₂ cup milk
1 egg, lightly beaten
1 tablespoon brown sugar
¹/₄ teaspoon ground cloves
¹/₂ cup pineapple juice
¹/₃ cup packed brown sugar
2 tablespoons lemon juice
1 tablespoon vinegar
6 slices canned pineapple, drained

Combine the ham, oats, milk, egg, 1 tablespoon brown sugar and ¹/₈ teaspoon of the cloves in a bowl and mix well. Shape into eighteen 1-inch balls.

Combine the pineapple juice, ¹/₃ cup brown sugar, lemon juice, vinegar and remaining ¹/₈ teaspoon cloves in a small saucepan. Simmer over medium heat for 8 to 10 minutes or until thickened, stirring occasionally.

Place the pineapple slices in a large skillet. Top each slice with 3 ham balls. Pour the pineapple sauce over the ham balls. Simmer, covered, over medium-low heat for 10 to 15 minutes or until heated through, basting occasionally with the pineapple sauce.

Serves Six

The Magic Hanky

I'm just a little hanky
As square as square can be,
But with a stitch or two
They make a bonnet out of me.

I'll be worn from the hospital
Or on the Christening Day,
Then I'll be carefully pressed
And neatly packed away.

For her wedding day
So we've been told,
Every well-dressed bride must have
That something old.

So what could be more fitting
Than to find little me,
A few stitches snipped
And a wedding hanky I'll be.

And if perchance, it is a BOY
Some day he'll surely wed,
So to the bride he can present
The hanky once worn on his head.

Champagne Chicken

1 cup flour
White pepper to taste
4 boneless skinless chicken breast halves
2 tablespoons sun-dried tomato oil
1¹/₂ cups Champagne or dry white wine
1 cup whipping cream
¹/₄ to ¹/₂ cup sliced sun-dried tomatoes

Combine the flour and white pepper in a shallow dish. Dip the chicken in the flour mixture, turning the pieces over to evenly coat both sides.

Heat the oil in a large skillet. Add the chicken. Cook until browned on 1 side; turn over. Stir in the oil and Champagne. Simmer over medium-low heat until the chicken is cooked through and the liquid is reduced by half. Remove the chicken from the skillet. Cover to keep it warm.

Stir the cream into the liquid in the skillet. Simmer until thickened, stirring frequently. Add the sun-dried tomatoes. Cook until heated through. Serve over the chicken.

Serves Four

Southwest Chicken Skillet

2 tablespoons vegetable oil
1 cup rice
1 teaspoon minced garlic
2 boneless skinless chicken breasts,
   cut into 1-inch pieces
2 cups chicken broth or water
1 (15-ounce) can ranch-style beans
2 green onions, sliced
1 cup shredded Cheddar cheese

Heat the oil in a large skillet over medium heat. Add the rice and garlic. Cook until lightly browned, stirring frequently. Add the chicken. Cook until the chicken is cooked through, stirring occasionally.

Reduce the heat to medium-low. Add the broth, undrained beans and green onions.

Simmer, covered, for 10 to 15 minutes or until the rice is tender and the liquid is absorbed, stirring occasionally. Sprinkle with the cheese. Cook, covered, until the cheese is melted.

Serves Two

Chicken with Capers

4 boneless skinless chicken breast halves
1 envelope instant chicken broth
1/3 cup olive oil
6 ounces fresh mushrooms, sliced
1/2 cup dry white wine
3 tablespoons capers

Pound the chicken to a 1/4-inch thickness. Sprinkle with the broth. Heat the oil in a large skillet over medium-high heat.

Add the chicken. Cook until golden brown on both sides and cooked through. Remove the chicken to a warmed serving platter, reserving the drippings in the skillet. Cover the chicken to keep it warm.

Add the mushrooms to the drippings in the skillet. Sauté for 30 to 40 seconds or until tender. Spoon over the chicken; cover.

Add the wine to the skillet. Bring to a boil; simmer over medium-low heat for 2 minutes or until the liquid is reduced by half. Add the capers. Cook until heated through. Spoon the sauce over the chicken.

Serves Three or Four

Baked Chicken with Rice

3 or 4 chicken breasts
2 onions, chopped
Vegetable oil
1 (10-ounce) can cream of mushroom
   soup
1 (10-ounce) can cream of celery soup
1 cup rice
1 (4-ounce) can sliced or whole
   mushrooms, drained

Cook the chicken in a nonstick skillet coated with nonstick cooking spray until browned on both sides. Remove from the skillet; set aside.

Sauté the onions in a small amount of oil in the same skillet until tender. Add the mushroom soup and celery soup and mix well. Stir in the rice. Spoon into a large casserole. Top with the chicken and mushrooms.

Bake at 350 degrees for 1½ hours.

Serves Three or Four

Curried Chicken

1/4 cup honey
3 tablespoons Dijon mustard
2 tablespoons melted butter
2 teaspoons curry powder
4 to 6 boneless skinless chicken breast
  halves

Combine the honey, mustard, butter and curry powder in a bowl.

Arrange the chicken in a single layer in a shallow baking pan. Pour the honey mixture over the chicken. Turn the chicken over to evenly coat both sides with the honey mixture.

Bake, uncovered, at 375 degrees for 20 minutes. Uncover. Bake for 10 minutes or until the chicken is cooked through. Place the chicken on a serving platter. Spoon the sauce over the chicken.

Serves Four to Six

Baked Mustard and Orange Chicken

3 pounds chicken quarters or parts
4 teaspoons Dijon mustard
1/2 cup finely chopped onion
2 tablespoons unsalted butter, cut into
  small pieces
Salt and pepper to taste
1 1/2 cups orange juice
1/4 cup packed dark brown sugar

Rinse the chicken and pat dry with paper towels. Coat the chicken with the mustard. Arrange skin side down in a single layer in a shallow roasting pan or baking dish. Top with the onion, butter, salt and pepper. Pour the orange juice around the chicken.

Bake at 375 degrees for 30 minutes, basting once. Turn the chicken skin side up. Sprinkle with the brown sugar.

Bake for 15 to 20 minutes or until the chicken is golden brown and cooked through, adding more orange juice to the pan if it becomes dry. Remove the chicken to a serving dish. Pour the pan juices into a small saucepan. Bring to a boil. Boil until thickened. Spoon over the chicken before serving.

Serves Four

TMC Babies

Everybody loves babies! Approximately four thousand babies are born each year at Tucson Medical Center. Our Auxilians help the mothers and families feel as comfortable as possible during this experience. Each baby receives a bonnet made from a white handkerchief trimmed in pink or blue. This is accompanied by "The Magic Hanky" poem. Both are often treasured through the years.

Our volunteers also provide a much-needed service by cuddling and rocking babies needing special attention. There is always a waiting list for this service.

At Christmas and Easter, the babies go home in special outfits designed and made by our "Sewing Ladies." The hospital loans going-home car seats when necessary. All babies must have car seats to be discharged. Our new Women's Center has beautiful, up-to-date birthing rooms. Through these many services, babies are assured a good start on their journey through life.

Company Chicken

1 (16-ounce) can whole cranberry sauce
1 (8-ounce) bottle French dressing
1 (1-ounce) envelope dry onion
   soup mix
6 to 8 boneless skinless chicken breast
   halves

Combine the cranberry sauce, dressing and soup mix in a bowl. Place the chicken in a shallow baking dish. Pour the cranberry sauce mixture over the chicken.

Refrigerate, covered, for 8 to 10 hours, occasionally spooning the cranberry sauce mixture over the chicken.

Bake, covered, at 350 degrees for 1 hour or until the chicken is cooked through.

Note: May refrigerate the baked chicken overnight and serve cold.

Serves Six to Eight

Crumbed Chicken Casserole

1 (7-ounce) package seasoned
   stuffing mix
1/2 cup melted butter
3 1/2 cups chopped cooked chicken
1 (10-ounce) can cream of mushroom
   soup
1 (4-ounce) can mushrooms
1/2 cup chicken stock
1/2 cup chopped onion
1/2 cup chopped celery
1/4 cup mayonnaise
1/8 teaspoon cayenne
Salt and pepper to taste
Sliced almonds (optional)

Combine the stuffing mix and butter in a bowl. Spoon half the stuffing mix mixture into a greased 5x9-inch baking dish.

Combine the chicken, mushroom soup, undrained mushrooms, chicken stock, onion, celery, mayonnaise, cayenne, salt and pepper in a bowl. Spoon into the prepared baking dish. Top with the remaining stuffing mixture. Sprinkle with the sliced almonds.

Bake at 325 degrees for 30 minutes or until bubbly.

Serves Eight to Ten

The Dinner Revolver

Raphael Pumpelly, an engineer headquartered at Tubac, Arizona, in the 1850s, arrived in Tucson after a grueling stagecoach trip and went in search of food: "I have no remembrance of having eaten for a week. So when I saw some men hurrying to a house where a man with a revolver stood ringing a bell, I turned to enter. The man stopped me. 'Fifty cents first' he said, holding out his hand. There were jerked beef, and beans and some things they called bread and coffee. You ate what was pushed to you; the memory of that pistol acted as a persuasion." He may have exaggerated just a bit.

Seared Turkey Tenderloin with Mango Pico de Gallo and Fried Prosciutto

1 cup finely diced peeled mango
¼ cup finely diced green onions
¼ cup finely diced red bell pepper
¼ cup finely diced husked tomatillos
2 teaspoons minced chipotle pepper
2 tablespoons chopped fresh cilantro
3 tablespoons lime juice
2 tablespoons olive oil
⅛ teaspoon salt
1 (1¼-pound) turkey tenderloin
½ cup flour
Salt and white pepper to taste
¼ cup clarified butter
4 thin slices prosciutto
Vegetable oil for deep-frying

Combine the mango, green onions, red pepper, tomatillos, chipotle pepper, cilantro, lime juice, olive oil and ⅛ teaspoon salt in a bowl. Refrigerate, covered, for 30 minutes.

Cut the turkey tenderloin diagonally into thin slices. Combine the flour, salt and white pepper in a shallow dish. Dredge the tenderloin slices in the seasoned flour. Sear in the clarified butter in a skillet or on a griddle until cooked through. Remove from the heat; keep warm.

Thread each prosciutto slice onto a metal skewer. Pour vegetable oil into a large saucepan to a depth of 4 inches. Heat until hot and add the skewers. Fry just until the prosciutto is crisp. Remove the prosciutto from the skewers.

Arrange the turkey slices on serving plates. Top with the mango pico de gallo. Arrange the fried prosciutto over the pico de gallo. Serve immediately.

Serves Four

Doubletree Hotel
Tom Gerlak, Executive Chef

Duck à l'Orange

1 (4¹/₂- to 5-pound) duckling, quartered
Salt and pepper to taste
1 (6-ounce) can frozen orange juice
    concentrate, thawed
1 (8-ounce) jar honey
¹/₂ cup water

Trim any excess skin from the duckling
pieces. Season the duckling with salt and
pepper. Place skin sides up in two 9x13-
inch baking dishes. Roast at 325 degrees
for 1 hour. Mix the orange juice concentrate,
honey and water in a bowl. Pierce the
duckling skins with a sharp knife. Turn the
pieces over. Pour the honey mixture over the
top. Roast for 1¹/₂ hours, turning the pieces
over every 30 minutes. Remove the
duckling pieces from the baking dishes.
Place skin sides up in shallow baking
dishes. Roast for an additional
15 minutes or until golden brown.

Serves Four

Salmon Delight

1 (16-ounce) can red salmon, drained
1 tablespoon lemon juice
1 tablespoon minced onion
Salt and pepper to taste
¹/₂ cup sour cream
Green bell pepper rings

Flake the salmon. Remove and discard any
pieces of skin and large bones. Place the
salmon in a small baking dish. Sprinkle with
the lemon juice, onion, salt and pepper.
    Top with spoonfuls of the sour cream.
Arrange the green pepper rings on top.
Bake, uncovered, for 20 minutes.

Serves Two or Three

Honey, Lime and Cilantro Grilled Salmon

2 cups mesquite honey
2 cups olive oil
1 cup lime juice
2 tablespoons chopped fresh cilantro
1 (6- to 7-ounce) salmon fillet
2 ripe papayas, peeled, seeded and diced
¼ each red, yellow and green bell pepper
4 green onions, chopped
¼ (or more) poblano chile, finely chopped
1 tablespoon chopped fresh cilantro
1 tablespoon unseasoned rice vinegar
1 teaspoon minced fresh garlic
Sugar and pepper to taste

Combine the honey, oil, lime juice and
2 tablespoons cilantro in a bowl. Mix until
well blended. Place the salmon in a shallow
baking dish. Top with the honey mixture.
Refrigerate, covered, for at least 2 hours.

For the salsa, combine the papayas, bell
peppers, green onions, poblano chile, 1
tablespoon cilantro, vinegar, garlic, sugar and
pepper in a bowl and mix well. Let the salsa
stand at room temperature for 1 hour.

Remove salmon from the marinade. Place
on a greased grill over medium coals. Grill
for about 5 minutes on each side or until the
salmon flakes easily. Serve with the salsa.

Serves Two

Tack Room
Alan Sanchez, Executive Chef

Stuffed Salmon for Four

2 to 3 tablespoons olive oil
1 bunch spinach leaves
3 garlic cloves, minced
Salt and pepper to taste
1 (2-pound) salmon fillet, skinned and
* boned*
1 (4-ounce) package goat cheese
Butter to taste
Lemon juice to taste
Dry white wine to taste

Heat the oil in a large skillet over medium-
high heat. Add the spinach and garlic. Cook
for 5 minutes or until the spinach is wilted
and tender, stirring occasionally; drain.
Season with salt and pepper.

Cut the salmon into 4 equal portions. Cut
a pocket in each portion, being careful not
to cut all the way through to the other side.

Combine the spinach and goat cheese in
a bowl. Spoon evenly into the pockets in
the salmon. Place the salmon in a shallow
baking pan. Season with salt and pepper,
butter, lemon juice and wine.

Bake at 350 degrees for 25 to 30 minutes
or until the salmon flakes easily.

Serves Four

Tanque Verde Guest Ranch
Mark Shelton, Executive Chef

129

Sea Bass with Citrus Relish

2 cups fish stock
4 or 5 threads saffron
4 garlic cloves, peeled, blanched and
    minced
2 tablespoons grated lemon peel
2 tablespoons grated orange peel
2 tablespoons snipped fresh chives
2 tablespoons finely chopped fresh
    parsley
1 shallot, peeled and minced
4 sea bass fillets

Combine the fish stock and saffron in a saucepan. Bring just to a boil. Remove the saucepan from the heat. Steep the saffron in the stock for 15 minutes. Strain the stock, discarding the saffron. Reheat the stock to a simmer.

Combine the garlic, lemon peel, orange peel, chives and parsley in a bowl. Spray the bottom of a large ovenproof skillet with nonstick cooking spray. Sprinkle the shallot over the bottom of the skillet. Add the bass fillets. Pour the stock over the bass. Cover with parchment paper.

Bake at 350 degrees for 15 minutes or until the bass flakes easily. Remove the bass from the liquid in the skillet. Place on a serving plate. Top with the herb mixture.

Note: May strain the cooking liquid and serve it with the cooked bass.

Serves Four

Tucson Medical Center
Todd Seligman, Executive Chef 1991–1996

Special Sole

4 large lemon sole fillets
Salt and pepper to taste
Garlic salt to taste
2 tablespoons butter
¼ cup finely chopped onion
¼ cup finely chopped mushrooms
¼ cup flour
¼ cup milk
¼ cup shredded sharp Cheddar cheese
Chopped cooked crab meat (optional)
½ cup dry white wine

Rinse the sole and pat dry. Sprinkle both sides of the sole lightly with salt, pepper and garlic salt. Melt the butter in a small skillet over medium-high heat. Add the onion and mushrooms. Cook until tender, stirring occasionally.

Combine the flour and milk in a small saucepan and mix well. Stir in the cheese. Cook over low heat until the cheese is melted, stirring constantly. Add the onion mixture. Cook for 3 to 4 minutes, stirring constantly. Season with salt and pepper.

Spoon the cheese sauce onto the centers of the sole fillets. Sprinkle with crab meat. Roll up the fillets. Place seam side down in a shallow baking dish. Pour the wine over the fillets. Bake at 350 degrees for 30 to 45 minutes or until the sole flakes easily.

Note: May substitute flaked canned crab meat for the chopped cooked crab meat.

Serves Four

Baked Seafood Casserole

1 cup mayonnaise
1 teaspoon Worcestershire sauce
½ teaspoon salt
⅛ teaspoon pepper
2 (7-ounce) cans shrimp, drained and
    flaked
1 (6-ounce) can crab meat, drained and
    flaked
1 (4-ounce) can chopped mushrooms,
    drained
1 medium green bell pepper, chopped
1 medium onion, chopped
1 cup finely chopped celery
Potato chips, crushed

Combine the mayonnaise, Worcestershire sauce, salt and pepper in a large bowl. Add the shrimp, crab meat, mushrooms, green pepper, onion and celery and mix lightly.

Spoon into a 1-quart baking dish or 6 individual baking shells. Sprinkle with potato chips.

Bake at 350 degrees for 25 minutes or until heated through.

Serves Six

Cioppino

1 tablespoon vegetable oil
1 medium green bell pepper, cut into
　½-inch pieces
2 tablespoons chopped onion
2 garlic cloves, minced
1 (14-ounce) can tomatoes, cut up
1 (8-ounce) can tomato sauce
½ cup dry white or red wine
3 tablespoons chopped fresh parsley
½ teaspoon salt
¼ teaspoon oregano
¼ teaspoon basil
⅛ teaspoon pepper
1 pound fresh or frozen fish fillets,
　cut up
1 pound peeled shrimp
2 (7-ounce) cans minced clams

Heat the oil in a large saucepan over medium-high heat. Add the green pepper, onion and garlic. Cook until the vegetables are tender but not brown, stirring occasionally. Add the undrained tomatoes, tomato sauce, wine, parsley, salt, oregano, basil and pepper.

Bring to a boil; reduce the heat to medium-low. Simmer, covered, for 20 minutes. Add the fish, shrimp and undrained clams. Return to a boil; reduce the heat to medium-low. Simmer for 10 minutes, stirring occasionally. Serve over hot cooked angel hair pasta.

Serves Six

Creamy Swiss and Crab Bake

1 1/2 cups sour cream
4 eggs, beaten
1/2 cup grated Parmesan cheese
1 teaspoon onion powder
1/4 teaspoon salt
4 drops of red pepper sauce
1 (6-ounce) can crab meat, drained and
    flaked
1 (4-ounce) can mushroom stems and
    pieces, drained
2 cups shredded Swiss cheese
1/4 cup flour

Combine the sour cream, eggs, Parmesan
cheese, onion powder, salt and red pepper
sauce in a large bowl and mix well. Stir in
the crab meat and mushrooms.

Combine the Swiss cheese and flour in
a bowl, mixing lightly to evenly coat the
cheese with the flour. Stir into the sour
cream mixture. Pour into an ungreased
10-inch pie plate.

Bake at 350 degrees for 45 minutes or
until a knife inserted in the center comes out
clean. Let stand for 5 minutes before cutting
into wedges to serve.

Note: May substitute 8 ounces chopped
imitation crab for the canned crab meat.

Serves Eight

Scallops

1 pound scallops
1 cup dry white wine
1 cup water
2 tablespoons butter
1/2 cup sliced mushrooms
1/2 cup chopped green bell pepper
2 green onions, sliced
3 tablespoons grated Parmesan cheese

Combine the scallops, wine and water in
a medium saucepan. Bring to a boil over
high heat; reduce the heat to medium-low.
Simmer for 10 minutes. Drain the scallops;
let cool. Place in a shallow baking pan.

Melt the butter in a medium skillet over
medium-high heat. Add the mushrooms,
green pepper and green onions.

Sauté for 5 minutes or until the vegetables
are tender. Spoon over the scallops. Sprinkle
with the Parmesan cheese.

Broil for 3 minutes or until the top is
bubbly and golden brown.

Serves Four

Shrimp Scorpio

3 tablespoons olive oil
2 cups finely chopped onions
1 garlic clove, minced
1/4 cup finely chopped fresh parsley
1/4 teaspoon dry mustard
1/4 teaspoon sugar
2 cups chopped peeled tomatoes
1/2 cup tomato sauce
1 pound shrimp (about 24), peeled,
    deveined
8 ounces feta cheese, crumbled

Heat the oil in a medium saucepan over medium-high heat. Add the onions and garlic. Cook until the onions are tender, stirring frequently. Stir in the parsley, dry mustard and sugar. Add the tomatoes and tomato sauce.

Simmer for 30 minutes, stirring occasionally. Rinse and drain the shrimp. Add to the tomato mixture. Simmer for 5 minutes.

Pour into a 1 1/2-quart baking dish. Sprinkle with the feta cheese.

Bake at 425 degrees for 10 to 15 minutes or until the cheese is melted. Serve immediately.

Serves Four

Skyline Country Club's Shrimp Diane St. Andrews

16 large unpeeled shrimp
1 tablespoon butter
10 medium mushrooms,
    cut into quarters
2 garlic cloves, minced
Seasoning Mix
$1/2$ cup dry white wine
$1/2$ cup Basic Shrimp Stock
$1/2$ cup sliced green onions
$4^1/2$ teaspoons butter, cut into
    small pieces

Peel the shrimp, reserving the shells for the Basic Shrimp Stock. Heat a large skillet over medium-high heat. Add the 1 tablespoon butter and the shrimp. Cook until the butter is melted, stirring frequently. Add the mushrooms and garlic. Cook until tender, stirring frequently.

Sprinkle about half the Seasoning Mix lightly over the shrimp mixture, stirring to coat evenly. (The more seasoning mix you use, the spicier the flavor.) Add the wine. Stir to scrape the browned bits off the bottom of the skillet. Add the Basic Shrimp Stock.

Simmer over medium-low heat until the liquid is reduced by half, stirring occasionally. Add the green onions and $4^1/2$ teaspoons butter. Turn off the heat. Shake the skillet gently to mix the ingredients in the skillet. Serve over hot cooked pasta or rice with crusty French bread slices.

Serves Two

Seasoning Mix

1 tablespoon paprika
$3/4$ teaspoon cayenne
1 teaspoon white pepper
1 teaspoon onion powder
$1/2$ teaspoon basil
$1/2$ teaspoon oregano
$1/2$ teaspoon thyme
$1/4$ teaspoon dry mustard
$1/4$ teaspoon salt

Combine the paprika, cayenne, white pepper, onion powder, basil, oregano, thyme, dry mustard and salt in a bowl. Mix well. Store in a cool, dry place.

Makes About Three Tablespoons

Basic Shrimp Stock

16 shrimp peels
2 cups water

Place the shrimp peels and water in a medium saucepan. Bring to a boil over high heat; reduce the heat to medium-low. Simmer until the liquid is reduced to $1/4$ cup. Strain the stock and let cool.

Makes One-Fourth Cup

Skyline Country Club
Issa Moussa, Executive Chef

TMC Auxiliary Courtesy Car

Anyone who has visited or worked at TMC knows that there are miles of hallways since the hospital is built on one level. To facilitate getting around this maze, the Auxiliary purchased a battery-operated Courtesy Car similar to the ones used in airport terminals. Volunteer drivers cheerfully take visitors and employees to any area within the hospital. All who use it are grateful for this convenience.

Canlis Shrimp

2 tablespoons butter
2 tablespoons olive oil
2 pounds peeled shrimp
¹/₂ teaspoon salt
¹/₄ teaspoon pepper
¹/₄ cup dry vermouth
2 tablespoons lemon juice

Melt the butter with the oil in a large skillet over medium heat. Add the shrimp. Season with the salt and pepper. Cook for 5 to 6 minutes or until the shrimp turn pink, stirring occasionally. Add the vermouth and lemon juice. Cook for 1 minute over high heat, stirring constantly. Serve with lemon wedges.

Serves Eight

Shrimp Catalina

Salt to taste
2 artichokes
2 lemons, cut into halves
1/2 cup dry white wine
1 tablespoon white wine vinegar
2 tablespoons chopped shallots
2 whole peppercorns
1 bay leaf
2 tablespoons whipping cream
1/2 cup unsalted butter, cut into
*   1-inch cubes*
1/4 teaspoon lemon juice
Pepper to taste
1 teaspoon olive oil
16 peeled and deveined shrimp
8 ounces button mushrooms
1/2 cup chopped tomato
1/2 cup minced green onions
2 tablespoons dry white wine

Fill a medium saucepan with salted water. Bring to a boil. Add the artichokes and lemons. Simmer over medium-low heat for 45 to 50 minutes or until the artichokes are tender but not fully opened; drain. Discard the lemons. Rinse the artichokes under cold running water to cool. Remove the hearts from the artichokes.

Remove and discard the beards from the bottoms and undersides of the artichoke hearts.

Combine the 1/2 cup wine, vinegar, shallots, peppercorns and bay leaf in a medium saucepan. Simmer over medium heat until the liquid is almost evaporated. Stir in the cream. Simmer until the liquid is thickened and reduced to a syrupy consistency. Add the butter. Cook over low heat until the sauce is smooth and coats a spoon, stirring constantly with a wire whisk. Stir in the lemon juice. Season with salt and pepper.

Heat the oil in a large skillet over high heat. Add the shrimp. Cook until the shrimp turn pink, stirring frequently. Add the mushrooms, tomato and green onions. Cook until the mushrooms are tender, stirring occasionally. Add the 2 tablespoons wine. Stir constantly to remove the glazed bits from the bottom of the pan. Remove from the heat. Cut the artichoke hearts into halves.

Place an artichoke half on each of 4 dinner plates. Top with the shrimp mixture and cream sauce.

Note: The lemons are added to the artichoke cooking water to help prevent the artichokes from darkening.

Serves Four

Anthony's
Stephan Michallet-Ferrier, Executive Chef

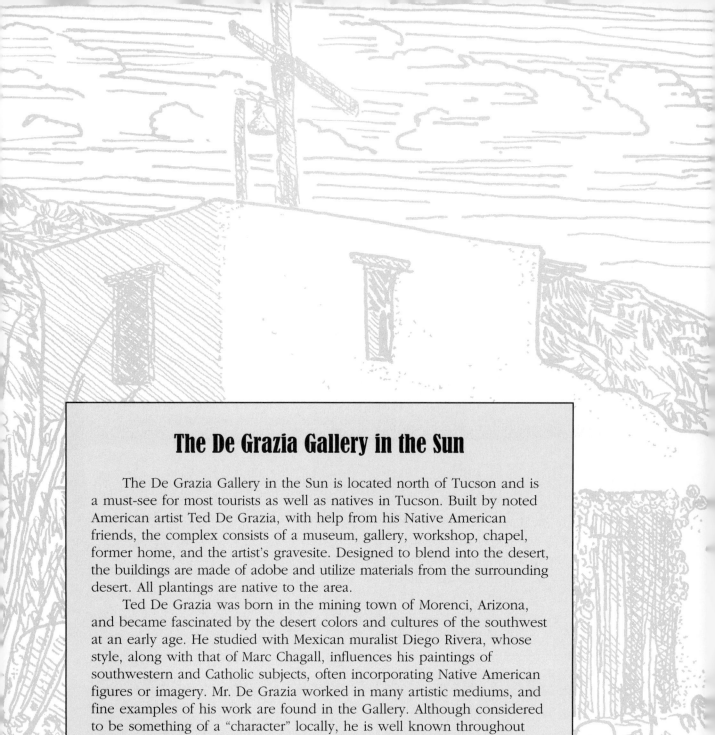

The De Grazia Gallery in the Sun

The De Grazia Gallery in the Sun is located north of Tucson and is a must-see for most tourists as well as natives in Tucson. Built by noted American artist Ted De Grazia, with help from his Native American friends, the complex consists of a museum, gallery, workshop, chapel, former home, and the artist's gravesite. Designed to blend into the desert, the buildings are made of adobe and utilize materials from the surrounding desert. All plantings are native to the area.

Ted De Grazia was born in the mining town of Morenci, Arizona, and became fascinated by the desert colors and cultures of the southwest at an early age. He studied with Mexican muralist Diego Rivera, whose style, along with that of Marc Chagall, influences his paintings of southwestern and Catholic subjects, often incorporating Native American figures or imagery. Mr. De Grazia worked in many artistic mediums, and fine examples of his work are found in the Gallery. Although considered to be something of a "character" locally, he is well known throughout the world and has many devoted collectors of his artwork.

Pasta & Rice

Gourmet Macaroni and Cheese

12 ounces elbow macaroni
2 quarts water
2 slices whole wheat bread
1/3 cup grated Parmesan cheese
1/4 teaspoon paprika
1 cup chopped onion
2 tablespoons water
1/4 cup flour
1/2 teaspoon paprika
2 cups evaporated milk
1 cup vegetable or chicken broth
3 cups shredded reduced-fat sharp
   Cheddar cheese
1/8 teaspoon nutmeg
Salt and pepper to taste

Cook the macaroni in 2 quarts boiling water in a medium saucepan for 6 to 8 minutes or just until tender; drain. Cover to keep warm.

Tear the bread into pieces. Place the bread, Parmesan cheese and 1/4 teaspoon paprika in a food processor or blender container. Process until the mixture forms coarse crumbs.

Place the onion and 2 tablespoons water in a large saucepan. Simmer over medium heat for 5 minutes or until the onion is tender and brown, stirring frequently.

Whisk in the flour and 1/2 teaspoon paprika. Remove from the heat. Blend in the evaporated milk and broth. Cook over high heat for 5 minutes or until the sauce boils, stirring constantly. Remove from the heat.

Add the Cheddar cheese, stirring until the cheese is melted. Stir in the nutmeg, salt and pepper.

Add the macaroni to the cheese sauce and mix well. Spoon into a lightly greased shallow 2- to 2 1/2-quart baking dish. Sprinkle with the bread crumb mixture.

Bake at 450 degrees for 3 to 4 minutes or until the topping is golden brown.

Serves Six to Eight

Fettuccini Alfredo

3 quarts water
1 tablespoon salt
8 ounces fettuccini
1/4 cup butter, softened
1/2 cup half-and-half
1/2 cup grated Parmesan cheese
Pepper to taste
Chopped fresh parsley

Place the water and salt in a large saucepan. Bring to a boil. Add the fettuccini. Return the water to a boil; reduce the heat to medium-low. Cook, uncovered, until the pasta is tender, stirring occasionally; drain. Return the pasta to the saucepan. Add the butter, half-and-half and Parmesan cheese and toss to mix. Season with pepper. Place the pasta mixture on a serving platter. Sprinkle with parsley.

Serves Six

Italian Mostaccioli and Cheese

8 ounces mostaccioli
Salt to taste
4 ounces Cheddar cheese,
*   cut into chunks*
1/2 medium onion, finely chopped
2 (8-ounce) cans tomato sauce
1 teaspoon onion powder
1 teaspoon garlic powder
Salt and pepper to taste
Grated Parmesan cheese

Cook the mostaccioli in lightly salted boiling water in a large saucepan for 8 minutes or just until tender; drain.

Place the mostaccioli in a large bowl. Add the Cheddar cheese and onion and mix well.

Combine the tomato sauce, onion powder and garlic powder in a medium saucepan. Simmer over medium-low heat for 5 minutes.

Season with salt and pepper. Pour the tomato sauce mixture over the mostaccioli and cheese and mix well. Spoon into a 9x13-inch baking dish. Sprinkle with Parmesan cheese.

Bake at 350 degrees for 20 minutes or until heated through.

Serves Eight

Noodle Pudding

8 ounces wide noodles
Salt to taste
3 eggs, beaten
1 cup sour cream
1/2 cup melted butter
1 tablespoon sugar
1/2 teaspoon salt
Sliced almonds (optional)

Cook the noodles in lightly salted boiling water in a large saucepan according to the package directions; drain. Place the noodles in a large bowl.

Combine the eggs, sour cream, butter, sugar, 1/2 teaspoon salt and almonds in a separate bowl and mix well. Add to the noodles and toss to mix.

Spoon into a greased 2-quart baking dish, about 1 1/2 inches deep. Bake at 325 degrees for 1 hour. Let stand for 10 minutes before serving. Cut into squares.

Note: This recipe can easily be doubled.

Serves Eight

The Chapel Window

Officially named The O.J. Farness, M.D. Memorial Stained Glass, this awesomely beautiful window, created by artist Jean Aspen, has drawn visitors from throughout the world. Forming the west wall of the Chapel, the window changes in intensity as the outside light changes throughout the day. The window combines many images with ancient trees, clouds, blue skies, mountains, and a ray of light that seems to transect the entire scene. Everyone who sees the window has a different interpretation of the scene, and therein lies the true beauty of this artistic treasure.

The TMC Chapel

The Chapel at Tucson Medical Center is situated on one of the busiest corridors in the hospital. However, when the door closes, one is aware only of solitude, peace, and tranquility.

Dedicated in 1985, the inter-faith chapel was funded by a substantial gift from the TMC Auxiliary and most generous donations from employees, persons in the community, and contributions from people in twenty-three states and several foreign countries.

With a forty-seat sanctuary, a meditation room, and a blessed sacrament room, the Chapel provides a special refuge for patients, visitors, and employees.

Noodles Delight

4 quarts water
4 nests of spinach pasta (ribbons)
4 tablespoons butter
1/2 cup finely chopped onion
2 cups stewed tomatoes
1 teaspoon basil
1 teaspoon parsley flakes
Salt and pepper to taste
1/2 cup whipping cream
1/4 cup grated Parmesan cheese

Bring the water to a boil in a large saucepan. Add the pasta. Cook according to the package directions until tender; drain. Place in a large bowl. Add 2 tablespoons of the butter and mix lightly. Cover to keep warm.

Melt the remaining 2 tablespoons butter in the same saucepan over medium-high heat. Add the onion. Cook until tender, stirring frequently. Add the tomatoes, basil and parsley and mix well. Season with salt and pepper.

Reduce the heat to medium-low. Cook for 5 minutes or until heated through, stirring occasionally. Stir in the whipping cream. Cook for 1 minute. Pour the sauce over the pasta and mix well.

Spoon into an 8x8-inch baking dish. Sprinkle with the Parmesan cheese. Broil for 5 minutes or until the top is golden brown.

Serves Four

Grandma's Beef and Noodles

1/4 cup vegetable oil
1 to 1 1/2 pounds very lean beef stew
    meat, cut into cubes
5 (14-ounce) cans chicken and/or
    vegetable broth
1 small onion, chopped
3 ribs celery, chopped
1/2 cup chopped celery leaves
1 teaspoon basil
Salt and pepper to taste
1 (12-ounce) package frozen egg noodles
1 pound mushrooms, sliced
Grated Parmesan cheese

Heat the oil in a large saucepan over medium-high heat. Add the beef. Cook until browned on all sides, stirring frequently. Add enough water to cover the beef. Reduce the heat to medium-low.

Simmer, covered, until tender. Add the broth, onion, celery, celery leaves, basil, salt and pepper. Bring to a boil. Add the noodles; reduce the heat to low. Simmer for 1 hour. Stir in the mushrooms. Simmer for 30 minutes. Sprinkle with Parmesan cheese.

Serves Eight to Ten

Orzo Casserole

2 garlic cloves, minced
3/4 cup vegetable oil
3 ripe tomatoes, chopped
1 medium green bell pepper, chopped
1 medium onion, chopped
1/2 cup chopped celery
1 pound orzo
2 cups water
Salt and pepper to taste
Crumbled feta cheese

Sauté the garlic in the oil in a medium saucepan over medium-high heat until golden. Add the tomatoes, green pepper, onion and celery.

Cook for 5 minutes or until the vegetables are tender, stirring frequently. Spoon into a 3-quart casserole. Add the orzo, water, salt and pepper and mix well.

Bake at 350 degrees for 1 hour or until the liquid is absorbed and the pasta is tender. Serve hot, sprinkled with feta cheese.

Serves Six to Eight

Italian Shells

16 large pasta shells
1 egg, beaten
16 ounces ricotta cheese
1/2 cup grated Parmesan cheese
1 (15-ounce) jar marinara or
    spaghetti sauce

Cook the pasta shells al dente in a large saucepan according to the package directions; drain. Cool.

Combine the egg, ricotta cheese and Parmesan cheese in a bowl and mix well.

Spoon the cheese filling evenly into the shells. Place the filled shells in a 9x13-inch baking dish. Pour the marinara sauce over the shells to cover.

Bake, covered, at 350 degrees for 30 minutes or until hot and bubbly.

Serves Four

Tucson Medical Center Art Treasures

Tucson Medical Center has a wealth of valuable paintings, stained glass windows, and other art forms. These have been donated by well-known local artists as well as "Sunday" painters. The hallways, lobbies, and offices are brightened by these generous gifts.

An outstanding example is the work of Chammatewa Buck, a Native American artist. Chamma came to TMC as an employee in the paint shop. He soon rose to foreman of the paint shop, but his true talent was recognized and he was appointed Resident Artist. In addition to his artwork for various in-house publications, Chamma created the design for the TMC Christmas card each year. His work stressed our Southwest heritage and his use of desert colors was widely admired. A project available for viewing

by everyone is the Hall of Shields located in the corridor beside the clinical laboratories. Sixteen circular shields are painted on the walls, each shield filled with symbols recognized by Indian tribes the world over. Chamma died in 1988, but he left a special legacy of art to TMC.

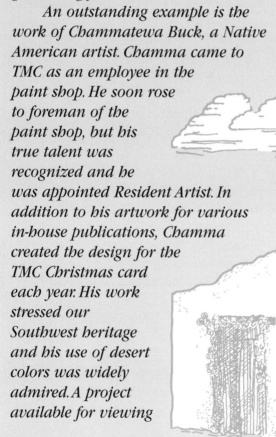

Talk About Tucson

People seem to have a love-it or hate-it relationship with Tucson. Those who love it tend to run on about the wonderful aspects of life in the desert. Those who hate it are equally vocal. A lady from New York made her opinions very clear in a letter to the editor of the Arizona Daily Star *in 1980: "After nearly three months in Tucson, one of the sunshine centers of the world, I am back in good, old, dull Rochester with its sleety weather and slippery pavements, its biting cold and dirty old December snow. And I couldn't like it better.... There, sand is the building material, houses hug the ground and have about them an impermanence that is shattering to one accustomed to the solidity of eastern cities. They are scattered all about like matchboxes blown around by the wind." She should give the city another chance!*

Rich and Dreamy Spaghetti

7 ounces spaghetti
3 tablespoons melted butter
1¹/₂ pounds ground beef
Salt and pepper to taste
2 (8-ounce) cans tomato sauce
8 ounces cream cheese, softened
1 cup small curd cottage cheese
¹/₄ cup sour cream
¹/₃ cup chopped onion, or 1 teaspoon onion powder
2 to 3 tablespoons chopped green bell pepper

Cook the spaghetti in a saucepan according to the package directions; drain. Place the spaghetti in a large bowl. Add the butter and toss to mix.

Brown the ground beef in a large skillet, stirring until crumbly; drain. Season with salt and pepper. Stir in the tomato sauce.

Combine the cream cheese, cottage cheese, sour cream, onion and green pepper in a bowl and mix well.

Place half the spaghetti in a 9x13-inch baking dish. Cover with the cream cheese mixture and the remaining spaghetti. Top with the ground beef sauce.

Refrigerate, covered, for 8 to 10 hours. Remove the baking dish from the refrigerator about 30 minutes before baking.

Bake, uncovered, at 350 degrees for 45 minutes or until hot and bubbly.

Serves Eight

Spaghetti Carbonara

1 pound spaghetti
8 ounces bacon slices, cut into
 1-inch pieces
1 small onion, finely chopped
1 garlic clove, minced
1/3 cup sweet vermouth
2 eggs, beaten
1/2 cup grated Parmesan cheese

Cook the spaghetti in a large saucepan
according to the package directions; drain.
Place the bacon, onion and garlic in a large
skillet. Cook over medium heat until the
bacon is crisp and the onion is tender,
stirring frequently; drain. Add the vermouth
and mix well.

Reduce the heat to medium-low. Simmer
for 3 to 4 minutes. Place the spaghetti in a
large bowl. Add the eggs and Parmesan
cheese, stirring to mix well. Stir in the bacon
mixture. Serve immediately.

Serves Four

Midwestern Chicken Macaroni Casserole

2 (10-ounce) cans cream of
    mushroom soup
1 cup milk
1 cup chicken broth
1 (7-ounce) package small elbow
    macaroni
2¹/₂ cups chopped cooked chicken
8 ounces Velveeta cheese, cubed
1 cup button mushrooms
1 small onion, finely chopped
2 hard-cooked eggs, chopped

Combine the soup, milk and broth in a large
bowl and mix well. Stir in the macaroni. Add
the chicken, Velveeta cheese, mushrooms,
onion and eggs and mix lightly.

Spoon into a 9x13-inch baking dish.
Refrigerate, covered, for 8 to 10 hours.
Remove from the refrigerator 1 hour
before baking.

Bake at 350 degrees for 1 hour or until
heated through. Let stand for 10 minutes
before serving.

Serves Ten

Angel Hair Pasta with Sautéed Shrimp

8 ounces angel hair pasta
4 tablespoons olive oil
1 teaspoon minced garlic
20 medium shrimp, peeled and deveined
2 (14-ounce) cans Italian-style stewed
    tomatoes, drained
¹/₂ cup dry white wine
¹/₄ cup chopped fresh parsley
3 tablespoons chopped fresh basil
Freshly grated Parmesan cheese

Cook the pasta in a large saucepan according
to the package directions; drain. Place the
pasta in a large bowl. Add 1 tablespoon of
the oil and mix lightly. Cover to keep warm.

Heat the remaining 3 tablespoons oil in a
large skillet over medium-high heat. Add the
garlic. Cook until tender, stirring frequently.
Stir in the shrimp. Cook until the shrimp turn
pink, stirring frequently. Remove the shrimp
from the skillet. Add the tomatoes, wine,
parsley and basil to the skillet.

Reduce the heat to medium-low. Simmer
for about 10 minutes or until the liquid is
reduced by half, stirring occasionally. Add
the shrimp. Cook until heated through,
stirring occasionally. Place the pasta on a
serving platter. Top with the shrimp mixture
and sprinkle with Parmesan cheese.

Note: May substitute 2 teaspoons dried basil
for the fresh basil.

Serves Six

One-Step Turkey and Rice Casserole

1 (10-ounce) can cream of
*   mushroom soup*
1¼ soup cans water
4 teaspoons Worcestershire sauce
1 pound ground turkey
1 cup long grain rice
1 small onion, chopped
½ medium bell pepper, chopped
1½ ribs celery, chopped

Combine the soup, water and Worcestershire sauce in a large bowl and mix well. Stir in the turkey, rice, onion, bell pepper and celery.

Spoon into a greased 2-quart baking dish. Bake at 350 degrees for 1 hour, adding additional water after 45 minutes if necessary.

Serves Four

Turkey and Ham Tetrazzini

7 ounces spaghetti
1/4 cup chopped green bell pepper
8 ounces mushrooms, sliced
1/4 cup butter
1/4 cup flour
1/4 teaspoon nutmeg
Salt and pepper to taste
1 (14-ounce) can chicken broth
1 cup milk
3 tablespoons dry sherry
2 cups cubed cooked turkey
1/2 cup cubed cooked ham
1 (4-ounce) can diced pimentos, drained
1 egg yolk
1/2 cup grated Parmesan cheese

Break the spaghetti into 2-inch pieces. Cook according to the package directions; drain. Place in a bowl; set aside.

Sauté the green pepper and mushrooms in a nonstick skillet coated with nonstick cooking spray until tender; set aside.

Melt the butter in a saucepan. Blend in the flour, nutmeg, salt and pepper. Cook over low heat until smooth and bubbly, stirring constantly. Remove from the heat. Stir in the broth and milk. Bring to a boil, stirring constantly. Boil for 1 minute, stirring constantly. Blend in the sherry. Pour over the spaghetti. Stir in the turkey, ham, green pepper, mushrooms, pimentos and egg yolk. Spoon into a 2-quart baking dish. Sprinkle with the Parmesan cheese.

Bake at 350 degrees for 25 to 30 minutes or until bubbly. Let stand for 10 minutes before serving.

Serves Six to Eight

Fitcenter A Program at Tucson Medical Center

The goal of this facility is to keep the Tucson community, especially the senior population, fit and healthy.

The exercise and therapy center covers 4500 square feet of space in the hospital proper, employs thirty-five instructors, and has 1800 participants in the various classes.

One can improve one's health either in the aerobic center, the pool, or the exercise room equipped with *the latest machines. One can exercise with a large group, a small group, or with a personal trainer. Oriental exercise disciplines are also offered.*

In spite of the occasional grunts and groans, this is a happy place where healthy results are documented every day.

Spanish Rice

1 pound fresh spinach
1 small onion, chopped
1/2 cup olive oil
1 1/2 cups water
2/3 cup rice
1 tablespoon chopped fresh dill
Salt and pepper to taste
Juice of 1 medium lemon

Wash the spinach; drain. Remove and discard the stems. Chop the leaves.

Sauté the onion in the oil in a medium saucepan until tender. Reduce the heat. Add the spinach and simmer until almost cooked through.

Add the water. Bring to a boil. Stir in the rice and the dill. Season with salt and pepper. Reduce the heat to medium-low.

Simmer, covered, for 15 minutes or until the rice is tender and the liquid is absorbed. Stir in the lemon juice.

Note: May substitute one 10-ounce package thawed frozen chopped spinach for the fresh spinach. To give the rice a tomato flavor, omit the lemon juice. Add 1/2 cup tomato sauce to the cooked onions. Continue as directed.

Serves Four or Five

A Few Passing Observations

James G. Bell, a military man from San Antonio, passed through Tucson in 1854. He made the following observation: "The women do the principal part of the work about the household; the men, long fellows with broad shoulders and no other part in proportion, seemed to be busily engaged in lounging." Some things never change. James Bell went on to say the soldiers were "a set of ragamuffins," the layout of the town was "very irregular," and the local priest was "only reported to have been drunk once since our stay— two days." It is doubtful that Bell was a regular visitor.

Rice Pilaf

1 cup converted rice
1½ cups chicken or beef broth
¼ cup melted butter
¼ cup water
1 cup sliced sautéed mushrooms
½ cup finely chopped celery
¼ cup slivered almonds

Combine the rice, broth, butter and water in a 2-quart baking dish. Bake, covered, at 300 degrees for 1 hour.

Add the mushrooms, celery and almonds. Bake, covered, for 20 minutes longer or until the liquid is absorbed and the rice is tender.

Note: Use chicken broth if you are serving this side dish with a chicken entrée and beef broth if you are serving a beef entrée.

Serves Six

Kitt Peak

Kitt Peak, an astronomical facility, is located fifty miles west of Tucson on the Tohono O'odham Indian reservation. At a height of 7000 feet, it is a prime location for astronomers to come and do research in the clear desert air. Approximately a dozen different telescopes are located here and astronomers come from all over the world to use these magnificent facilities.

The headquarters of this "heavenly" operation are located near the University of Arizona. Much of the research is now done by computer, and the engineering support system located "down below" facilitates much of the research done "up above."

Visitors are welcome and special tours can be arranged. The city of Tucson has legislated that all outdoor illumination be shielded from above. As a result of these laws, the skies are much clearer for Tucsonans as well as for the scientists atop Kitt Peak.

Vegetables & Sides

Baked Beans

1 (31-ounce) can pork and beans
¹/₄ cup catsup
2 tablespoons bacon drippings (optional)
2 tablespoons brown sugar
1 tablespoon Worcestershire sauce
3 drops of Tabasco sauce
Salt to taste
3 or 4 slices bacon, cut into 1-inch pieces
Chopped onion
Chopped celery
Chopped green bell pepper

Combine the pork and beans, catsup, bacon drippings, brown sugar, Worcestershire sauce, Tabasco sauce and salt in a bowl and mix well. Stir in the bacon, onion, celery and green pepper. Spoon into a 2-quart baking dish.

Bake at 375 degrees for 30 minutes or until hot and bubbly.

Note: This makes a great side dish when cooked on the grill. Cook in a cast-iron skillet over medium coals until hot and bubbly.

Serves Four to Six

Cowgirl Bean Casserole

4 to 6 slices bacon
1 cup chopped yellow onion or
    green onions
1 medium green bell pepper, chopped
2 ribs celery, chopped
2 garlic cloves, chopped
1 (31-ounce) can pork and beans
1 (15-ounce) can pinto beans with
    jalapeños
1 (15-ounce) can pinto beans
1 (15-ounce) can kidney beans
1 (15-ounce) can navy beans
1 (15-ounce) can butter beans
1 (20-ounce) can pineapple tidbits
2 tablespoons brown sugar
2 tablespoons each catsup, chili sauce
    and mustard
4 or 5 whole cloves

Cook the bacon in a large heavy skillet until crisp; remove the bacon and drain on paper towels. Crumble and set aside.

Sauté the onion, green pepper, celery and garlic in the bacon drippings until tender; set aside.

Pour the pork and beans, pinto beans, kidney beans, navy beans and butter beans with half their liquid into an ovenproof Dutch oven. Add the crumbled bacon, sautéed vegetables, undrained pineapple, brown sugar, catsup, chili sauce, mustard and cloves. Stir until well mixed.

Bake at 225 degrees for 1½ hours or until hot and bubbly.

Serves Ten to Twelve

Grecian Green Beans

½ cup olive oil
1 large onion, chopped
2 garlic cloves, minced
1 (15-ounce) can stewed tomatoes
2 (9-ounce) packages frozen green
    beans, thawed
1 (8-ounce) can tomato sauce
1 teaspoon dillweed
½ teaspoon garlic powder
Salt and pepper to taste

Heat the oil in a large skillet over medium-high heat. Add the onion and garlic. Cook until tender, stirring frequently.

Break the stewed tomatoes into pieces. Add the tomatoes, green beans, tomato sauce, dillweed and garlic powder to the skillet. Season with salt and pepper.

Bring to a boil; reduce the heat to medium-low. Simmer for 25 minutes, stirring occasionally.

Serves Five or Six

Gambel's Quail

Gambel's Quail are smile producers. They are ground birds, gray in color with brown and white streaking. Most striking is the forward curving black topknot. The males have a russet crown while the females are more buff colored. Very family oriented, the parents and the chicks travel in a group with mother leading the way and father acting as a sentinel at the rear. When newly hatched, the chicks resemble puffballs but are able to walk right away. It is not unusual to see twelve or fourteen chicks in a family, but survival is a struggle in the desert and families are often decimated by predators.

Beets in Maple Orange Sauce

6 medium fresh beets (about 2 pounds)
1 medium onion
1/4 cup maple syrup
2 tablespoons unsweetened orange juice
1/2 teaspoon dry mustard
1/2 teaspoon grated orange peel
1/8 teaspoon salt
1/8 teaspoon pepper

Trim the root end from each beet and all but 1 inch of the stem; scrub the beets. Wrap each beet and the onion separately in foil.

Place in a shallow baking dish. Bake at 375 degrees for 1 1/4 hours; cool. Unwrap the vegetables.

Trim the remaining stems off the beets and rub off the skins. Cut the beets into julienne strips.

Peel the onion; cut into 1/4-inch-thick slices. Cut each onion slice crosswise into halves.

Combine the maple syrup, orange juice, dry mustard, orange peel, salt and pepper in a large nonstick skillet and mix well. Cook over medium heat until the mixture comes to a simmer, stirring frequently. Stir in the beets and onion. Cook for 2 minutes or until heated through, stirring constantly.

Serves Four

English Walnut Broccoli

2 (10-ounce) packages frozen chopped broccoli
1/2 cup butter
1/4 cup flour
4 chicken bouillon cubes, crushed
2 cups milk
2/3 cup water
6 tablespoons butter
2 cups herb-seasoned stuffing mix
2/3 cup chopped walnuts

Cook the broccoli in a medium saucepan according to the package directions; drain. Spoon into a 1 1/2-quart greased baking dish.

Melt the 1/2 cup butter in a large skillet over medium-low heat. Blend in the flour and crushed bouillon cubes. Add the milk gradually, stirring constantly. Cook until thickened, stirring frequently. Pour over the broccoli.

Place the water and 6 tablespoons butter in a medium saucepan. Heat until the butter is melted. Pour into a medium bowl. Add the stuffing mix and mix lightly. Stir in the walnuts. Spoon over the broccoli mixture, spreading with the back of a spoon to completely cover the top. Bake at 350 degrees for 30 minutes.

Serves Eight

Gila Woodpecker

This bird, common to the desert, is very visible, very active, and very audible. It has a black and white zebra-striped back and wears a red cap. It usually makes its presence felt by drilling holes in eaves and vigas of homes and in the stately saguaro cactus. During mating season, it attracts the female by pecking on metal objects such as chimney caps, often early in the morning.

Fez Carrots

1/2 cup seedless raisins
2 bunches carrots (about 2 pounds)
1/2 medium onion
6 tablespoons butter
1/4 cup dry white wine
1/2 teaspoon nutmeg
2 tablespoons brown sugar

Place the raisins in a small bowl. Add enough boiling water to cover. Let stand until the raisins are plumped; drain.

Cut the carrots into 1/4-inch slices and the onion into very thin slices. Melt the butter in a large saucepan. Add the carrots, onion, wine and nutmeg and mix lightly. Cook, covered, for 20 minutes or until the carrots are tender, stirring occasionally.

Stir the raisins and brown sugar into the carrots. Cook until heated through.

Note: May substitute frozen carrots for the fresh carrots.

Serves Six to Eight

Corn Pudding

1 egg
1 cup sour cream
1 (15-ounce) can whole kernel corn
1 (15-ounce) can cream-style corn
1 (8-ounce) package corn bread mix
1/2 cup melted butter

Beat the egg in a small bowl. Combine the egg and sour cream in a medium bowl and mix well. Stir in the undrained whole kernel corn and cream-style corn.

Add the corn bread mix and stir just until moistened. Stir in the butter. Spoon into a greased 1½-quart baking dish. Bake at 350 degrees for 1 hour or until set.

Serves Six to Eight

Corn and Green Chile Casserole

3 large eggs
2 tablespoons milk
1 cup sour cream
1/2 cup melted butter
1 (8-ounce) can cream-style corn
1 (10-ounce) package frozen whole
   kernel corn, thawed
1 (4-ounce) can chopped green chiles
1/4 teaspoon Worcestershire sauce
1 cup shredded Monterey Jack cheese
1 cup shredded sharp Cheddar cheese
1/2 cup yellow cornmeal
1/2 teaspoon salt

Whisk the eggs and milk in a large bowl. Blend in the sour cream and butter. Stir in the cream-style corn, whole kernel corn, green chiles and Worcestershire sauce. Add the Monterey Jack cheese, Cheddar cheese, cornmeal and salt and mix lightly. Spoon into a greased 1½-quart casserole.

Bake at 350 degrees for 1 hour or until firm to the touch.

Note: This baked casserole freezes nicely.

Serves Six

Papagayo's Green Corn Tamale Casserole

2 (4-ounce) cans whole green chiles
3 eggs, separated
1½ cups milk, scalded
1 cup white cornmeal
¾ teaspoon salt
1 (16-ounce) can cream-style white corn
¾ cup large curd cottage cheese
3 tablespoons melted butter
1 teaspoon baking powder
2 cups shredded longhorn cheese

Drain the green chiles and cut into strips; set aside. Beat the egg whites in a mixer bowl until stiff peaks form. Beat the egg yolks in a separate small bowl until thick and pale yellow.

Combine the milk, cornmeal and salt in a medium saucepan. Cook over low heat until the mixture is thickened, stirring constantly.

Add the corn, cottage cheese, butter and baking powder and mix well. Fold in the egg yolks and then the egg whites. Layer the batter, cheese and green chiles in a greased 2-quart casserole until all the ingredients are used, ending with the batter.

Bake at 375 degrees for 40 minutes or until set.

Note: May use egg substitute instead of the fresh eggs. Do not beat the egg substitute.

Serves Six

Baked Eggplant

1 large eggplant (about 2 pounds)
Salt to taste
$1/2$ cup saltine cracker crumbs
$1/2$ teaspoon paprika
$1/2$ teaspoon salt
$1/4$ teaspoon oregano
1 egg
1 tablespoon water
$1/4$ cup melted butter

Peel the eggplant; cut into $1/2$-inch-thick slices. Cut each slice crosswise into halves. Place in a large bowl. Add enough cold salted water to cover. Let stand at room temperature for 30 minutes. Drain the eggplant; pat dry with paper towels.

Combine the cracker crumbs, paprika, $1/2$ teaspoon salt and oregano in a shallow dish. Whisk the egg with the water in a separate bowl. Dip the eggplant slices into the egg. Coat the slices with the cracker crumb mixture, turning the slices to evenly coat both sides.

Arrange the eggplant in a greased 6x10-inch baking dish. Let stand at room temperature for 30 minutes. Drizzle with the butter.

Bake at 400 degrees for 20 minutes or until the eggplant is tender.

Serves Four

Hummingbirds

The hummingbird is not only the smallest bird in the world but one of the most interesting. There are hundreds of varieties and some sixteen are found in the Sonoran Desert. They vary in size and coloring and have a long needle-like bill for probing into flowers and an incredibly long tongue that protrudes beyond the bill to secure nectar.

The hummingbird flight pattern is unique, since hummingbirds possess the ability to hover, fly sideways, and fly in circles. The wings beat so fast that they appear to blur. With a very high metabolism, the hummingbird must feed often, as much as three hundred times a day. At night, it goes into a trance-like state and lowers its metabolism.

Hummingbirds are very territorial and dive-bomb other birds at their feeding station. The male hummingbird is a hopeless romantic and royally woos his lady with fancy flying that shows off his coloring. A hummingbird feeder outside a window can provide hours of enjoyment for the mere humans who watch from inside.

Deluxe Creamed Onions

1½ pounds pearl onions, peeled
2 tablespoons butter or margarine
2 tablespoons flour
¼ teaspoon salt
⅛ teaspoon white pepper
1 cup half-and-half or milk

Combine the onions and butter in a 1½-quart microwave-safe baking dish.

Microwave on High for 7 to 10 minutes or until the onions are tender, stirring after 5 minutes.

Add the flour, salt and pepper and mix well. Stir in the half-and-half.

Microwave, uncovered, for 2 to 5 minutes or until the mixture comes to a boil, stirring after 2 minutes. Stir well and serve hot.

Serves Four to Six

Cauliflower Tomato Au Gratin

2 (16-ounce) packages frozen
   cauliflower
3/4 cup shredded American cheese
4 to 5 tablespoons butter
2 medium onions, diced
5 sprigs of fresh parsley
1 (14-ounce) can stewed tomatoes
1/3 cup dry bread crumbs
   (about 1 1/2 slices bread)
2 bouillon cubes
2 tablespoons sugar
1 teaspoon salt
1/8 teaspoon pepper
1/4 cup shredded American cheese

Cook the cauliflower in a large saucepan
according to the package directions; drain.
Place in a large bowl. Add 3/4 cup cheese
and toss lightly.

Melt the butter in a large skillet. Add the
onions and parsley. Cook until the onions
are tender, stirring frequently. Add the
tomatoes, bread crumbs, bouillon cubes,
sugar, salt and pepper and mix well. Cook
over medium-low heat for 5 minutes, stirring
occasionally.

Spoon half the tomato mixture into a
greased 2-quart baking dish. Top with the
cauliflower mixture and the remaining
tomato mixture. Sprinkle with 1/4 cup cheese.

Bake, covered, for 15 minutes. Uncover.
Bake for 15 minutes longer.

Serves Twelve

Yum-Yum Potatoes

6 to 8 potatoes
1 (10-ounce) can cream of chicken
   soup
1 cup shredded Cheddar cheese
1 cup sour cream
1/2 cup shredded Cheddar cheese
1 teaspoon basil

Cook the potatoes in a large saucepan of
boiling water for 30 to 40 minutes or until
tender; drain and cool. Cut the potatoes into
1/8-inch-thick slices. Place in a greased 9x13-
inch baking dish.

Combine the soup and 1 cup cheese in a
medium saucepan. Cook over medium heat
until the cheese is melted, stirring constantly.
Remove from the heat. Stir in the sour cream.

Pour evenly over the potatoes. Sprinkle
with 1/2 cup cheese and basil.

Bake at 350 degrees for 30 minutes.

Serves Six

Greater Roadrunner

This Arizona bird is a large, slender, streaked cuckoo. He sports a long white-edged tail and long powerful legs. Predominately a ground bird, he spends much of his time searching for his next meal of bugs, small reptiles, and quail eggs. His loud squawking call alerts other birds to his impending arrival.

Caraway Potatoes

¹/₄ cup butter
2 tablespoons minced onion
2 tablespoons caraway seeds
1 teaspoon salt
¹/₂ teaspoon paprika
¹/₄ teaspoon pepper
2 (16-ounce) cans small potatoes, drained

Place the butter in a 6x10-inch baking dish. Place in a 350-degree oven. Heat until the butter is melted. Remove from the oven. Stir in the onion, caraway seeds, salt, paprika and pepper. Add the potatoes and mix well.

Bake for 30 minutes or until heated through.

Note: To make ahead, prepare the recipe as directed except for baking. Refrigerate, covered, until ready to bake.

Serves Six

Mashed Potato with Carrots and Caramelized Onion

1 teaspoon butter
1 small onion, chopped
1 large Idaho baking potato, peeled
2 medium carrots, peeled
1/4 cup ricotta cheese
1/4 teaspoon salt

Melt the butter in a small skillet over medium-high heat. Add the onion. Cook for 8 to 10 minutes or until golden brown, stirring frequently; set aside.

Cut the potato and carrots into pieces. Add to a large saucepan of boiling water. Cook for 8 to 10 minutes or until the vegetables are tender; drain well.

Mash the potato and carrots together until the carrots are in small chunks. Beat in the onion, ricotta cheese and salt.

Serves Two

Sweet Potato Casserole

10 cups (about) water
*6 large sweet potatoes, peeled and
    cut into chunks*
1/4 cup butter
2 eggs, lightly beaten
1/2 cup milk
1/2 teaspoon vanilla extract
1/2 cup sugar
1/2 teaspoon salt
Miniature marshmallows (optional)

Bring the water to a boil in a large saucepan. Add the sweet potatoes. Cook over medium-low heat for 20 minutes or until the sweet potatoes are tender; drain well. Return the sweet potatoes to the saucepan. Mash slightly.

Add the butter, eggs, milk, vanilla, sugar and salt, mixing until well blended. Spoon into a greased 2-quart casserole. Top with a layer of marshmallows.

Bake at 350 degrees for 35 to 45 minutes or until heated through.

Note: May sprinkle the top of the casserole with light brown sugar instead of the marshmallows before baking.

Serves Six

Biosphere II

Every creature on Earth is acquainted with Biosphere I. This is the ground we walk on, the air we breathe, and every living thing associated with earth and sky. However, only those persons who travel 25 miles north of Tucson and turn off Highway 77 onto Biosphere Road will encounter Biosphere II. This is a three-acre, enclosed ecological system managed by Columbia University. There is a tropical rain forest, a savannah, a desert, a marsh, and an ocean with a coral reef. This human habitat, once occupied by fifteen "Biospherians," has been transformed into a Science Center dedicated to the Earth and environmental sciences. Visitors are welcome to tour the facility, with private tours and educational workshops available. It is a most interesting way to spend a day.

Lentils and Rice

1 cup lentils
8 cups water
1 cup rice
Salt and pepper to taste
1/4 cup olive oil
2 large onions, chopped

Sort and rinse the lentils in cold water.
Bring the 8 cups water to a boil in a medium
saucepan. Add the lentils.

Reduce the heat to medium-low. Simmer
for 20 minutes. Add the rice, salt and pepper.
Simmer for 15 minutes.

Heat the olive oil in a small skillet.
Add the onions. Cook until tender, stirring
frequently. Add to the lentil mixture and
mix well.

Serves Six to Eight

Spaghetti Squash Monterey

1 spaghetti squash
1/4 cup butter
1 large onion, chopped
1/2 cup sour cream
Salt and pepper to taste
2 cups shredded Monterey Jack cheese
Paprika to taste

Cut the squash lengthwise into halves;
remove and reserve the seeds for another
use. Place the squash halves cut side down
in a large saucepan filled with 2 inches
of water; cover. Bring to a boil. Boil for
20 minutes. Remove the squash pulp from
the shells with a fork. Place the spaghetti-like
strands in a large bowl.

Melt the butter in a large skillet. Add the
onion. Cook until tender, stirring frequently.
Add to the squash along with the sour
cream, salt and pepper and mix well. Stir in
1 cup of the cheese.

Spoon into a greased 2-quart casserole.
Top with the remaining 1 cup cheese.
Sprinkle with paprika. Bake at 325 degrees
for 30 minutes.

Note: For an impressive buffet dish, bake
and serve this side dish in the spaghetti
squash shells.

Serves Six to Eight

John Wayne Cheese Casserole

2 (4-ounce) cans whole green chiles,
    drained, seeded
4 cups shredded Monterey Jack cheese
4 cups shredded Cheddar cheese
4 eggs, separated
1 (5-ounce) can evaporated milk
1 tablespoon flour
1/2 teaspoon salt
1/8 teaspoon pepper
2 medium tomatoes, sliced

Chop the green chiles and place them in a large bowl. Add the Monterey Jack cheese and Cheddar cheese and mix lightly. Spoon into a greased shallow 2-quart casserole.

Beat the egg whites in a mixer bowl until stiff peaks form. Whisk the egg yolks and evaporated milk in a bowl until well blended. Stir in the flour, salt and pepper. Fold the egg whites into the egg yolk mixture. Pour over the cheese mixture in the casserole.

Pierce the layers with a fork to allow the cheese mixture to absorb some of the egg mixture.

Bake at 325 degrees for 30 minutes. Remove from the oven. Arrange the tomato slices around the edge of the casserole. Bake for 30 minutes longer or until a knife inserted in the center comes out clean.

Serves Eight

Cheesy Vegetable Casserole

*1 (16-ounce) package frozen chopped
    broccoli, thawed*
Grated Parmesan cheese to taste
2 eggs, beaten
8 ounces mushrooms, sliced and sautéed
1 medium zucchini, sliced
1 (14-ounce) can stewed tomatoes
Oregano to taste
1 (10-ounce) can Cheddar cheese soup

Place the broccoli in a 9x13-inch greased
casserole. Sprinkle with Parmesan cheese.

Pour the eggs over the cheese. Layer the
mushrooms, zucchini and tomatoes over the
top. Season with the oregano.

Spoon the soup over the tomatoes,
spreading to cover. Sprinkle with additional
Parmesan cheese.

Bake at 350 degrees for 40 minutes or
until heated through.

Serves Six

Ratatouille Pie

¼ cup butter or margarine
1 cup chopped zucchini
1 cup chopped peeled eggplant
½ cup chopped tomato
½ cup chopped green bell pepper
¼ cup chopped onion
1 garlic clove, minced
¾ teaspoon salt
½ teaspoon basil
⅛ teaspoon pepper
1 cup shredded Monterey Jack cheese
3 eggs
1¼ cups milk
¼ cup sour cream
¾ cup baking mix

Melt the butter in a large skillet over medium
heat. Add the zucchini, eggplant, tomato,
green pepper, onion and garlic. Cook over
medium heat for 5 to 10 minutes or until the
vegetables are tender-crisp, stirring frequently.
Stir in the salt, basil and pepper. Spoon the
mixture into a lightly greased 10-inch pie
plate. Sprinkle with the cheese.

Whisk the eggs and milk in a medium
bowl until blended. Stir in the sour cream.
Add the baking mix and mix well. Pour over
the vegetables and cheese in the pie plate.

Bake at 400 degrees for 30 to 35 minutes
or until golden brown.

Note: The vegetable amounts do not have to
be exact.

Serves Four to Six

The Arizona-Sonora Desert Museum

The Arizona-Sonora Desert Museum is a world-renowned desert park featuring live species of animals, fish, and plants native to the Sonoran Desert region of Arizona, the Mexican state of Sonora, and the Gulf of California. In 1982, *The New York Times* described it as one of the best zoos in the world and probably the most distinctive in the United States.

All the animals are viewed in their natural habitat, with snakes separated from visitors by glass. An Earth Science Center, a man-made cave, and a world-class mineral exhibit enthrall visitors. There is also a walk-through aviary for viewing desert birds, a walk-in hummingbird exhibit, and an underground viewing station for watching the antics of otters and beavers. Cats, bears, foxes, and mountain goats can all be found on the grounds.

Water fountains and shady ramadas, as well as helpful docents, make this a welcoming, delightful place for the many thousands who visit each year.

Desserts

Grandma's Apple Cake

1 cup shortening
1 cup sugar
1 cup packed brown sugar
2 eggs
2 cups cake flour, sifted
2 teaspoons baking soda
1 teaspoon salt
2 teaspoons cinnamon
2 teaspoons nutmeg
4 cups diced apples
Chopped walnuts or pecans (optional)

Cream the shortening, sugar and brown sugar in a mixer bowl until light and fluffy. Beat in the eggs.

Sift the cake flour, baking soda, salt, cinnamon and nutmeg together. Add the dry ingredients to the egg mixture and mix well. The batter will be very thick. Stir in the apples.

Spoon into a greased 9x13-inch baking dish. Sprinkle walnuts over the top.

Bake at 350 degrees for 45 minutes or until a wooden pick inserted in the center comes out clean. Serve warm with ice cream if desired.

Serves Ten to Twelve

Cherry Cake

3/4 cup butter, softened
1 cup sugar
3 eggs
1/4 cup sour cream
2 cups flour
1 teaspoon baking soda
1 teaspoon cinnamon
1 teaspoon ground cloves
1/4 teaspoon nutmeg
1 (16-ounce) can pitted tart cherries, drained

Cream the butter and sugar in a mixer bowl until light and fluffy. Beat in the eggs and sour cream.

Add the flour, baking soda, cinnamon, cloves and nutmeg and mix well. Stir in the cherries.

Spoon into a greased 9x13-inch pan.

Bake at 375 degrees for 25 minutes or until a wooden pick inserted in the center comes out clean. Cool in the pan on a wire rack. Spread with desired frosting.

Serves Fifteen

Apple Oatmeal Crumb Cake

1 cup flour
1/3 cup rolled oats
1/3 cup sugar
1/3 cup packed dark brown sugar
1/8 teaspoon salt
1/8 teaspoon ground nutmeg
1/4 cup cold butter or margarine,
    cut into small pieces
1/3 cup apple juice
1 egg
1 teaspoon vanilla extract
1/2 teaspoon baking powder
1/4 teaspoon baking soda
1 1/2 cups chopped peeled McIntosh or
    other firm apples

Combine the flour, oats, sugar, brown sugar, salt and nutmeg in a mixer bowl. Cut in the butter until the mixture resembles coarse crumbs. Reserve 1/2 cup of the crumb mixture.

Add the apple juice, egg, vanilla, baking powder and baking soda to the remaining crumb mixture. Beat at medium speed until blended. Fold in the apples. Spoon into an 8-inch round cake pan sprayed with nonstick cooking spray. Sprinkle the reserved crumb mixture over the top.

Bake at 350 degrees for 30 minutes or until the cake springs back when lightly touched. Cool in the pan on a wire rack.

Serves Eight

Tucson Medical Center Urgent Care

Patients have always been able to receive urgent care at TMC, but often endured long waits in the Emergency Room while major traumas and serious illnesses were treated first. This was hard to explain to waiting patients since all think their problems are urgent.

In 1987, a walk-in clinic was established in the ER to treat people with non-life-threatening illnesses. This service was available from 5 to 11 p.m. weekdays and 8 a.m. to 11 p.m. weekends. It proved to be a very busy area so, in 1992, a separate modular building was erected on the west side of the hospital, staffed by a physician, a nurse, and a technician. Staff increases were soon necessary as 12,000 patients were seen in the first year of operation.

When the Emergency Services area was renovated in 1995, Urgent Care finally had a permanent home. The modern facility has state-of-the-art equipment and a full staff that rarely sees a dull day. Triage duties are shared with the ER so that patients can be easily transferred between the two areas. In 1997, 30,000 patients were seen in Urgent Care.

A courtesy desk staffed by Auxilians and paid staff was established in 1998. The volunteers greet patients and their families and circulate between the lobby and the treatment areas. They can arrange for family members to visit the patient or provide up-to-the-minute information about the patient. They also spend time with all patients to make sure their stay is a positive experience.

Chocolate Bar Bundt Cake

1 cup butter, softened
2 cups sugar
4 eggs
5 ounces chocolate syrup
1 teaspoon vanilla extract
1 cup buttermilk
¹/₂ teaspoon baking soda
2¹/₂ cups sifted cake flour
6 ounces milk chocolate candy bars,
    melted
1 cup sugar
1 egg yolk
3 tablespoons brandy
1 cup whipping cream, whipped
Confectioners' sugar

Cream the butter and the 2 cups sugar in a mixer bowl until light and fluffy. Add the 4 eggs 1 at a time, beating well after each addition. Beat in the chocolate syrup and vanilla.

Combine the buttermilk and baking soda in a measuring cup. Add to the butter mixture alternately with the flour. Stir in the melted candy bars and mix well. Pour into a greased bundt pan.

Bake at 325 degrees for 1 hour. Cool in the pan for 5 minutes. Remove from the pan and cool completely on a wire rack.

Combine the 1 cup sugar, egg yolk and brandy in a bowl, beating well. Fold in the whipped cream. Dust the top of the cake with confectioners' sugar. Serve with the brandy sauce.

Serves Sixteen

Chocolate Pound Cake

1 cup butter, softened
1/2 cup shortening
3 cups sugar
5 eggs
3 cups flour
1/2 cup baking cocoa
1/2 teaspoon baking powder
1/4 teaspoon salt
1 1/4 cups milk
1 teaspoon vanilla extract
1 cup packed brown sugar
1/4 cup milk
2 tablespoons butter
2 tablespoons shortening
1 teaspoon vanilla extract
Confectioners' sugar

Cream the 1 cup butter, 1/2 cup shortening and sugar in a mixer bowl until light and fluffy. Add the eggs 1 at a time, beating well after each addition.

Sift the flour, cocoa, baking powder and salt together 3 times. Add to the butter mixture alternately with the 1 1/4 cups milk. Beat in 1 teaspoon vanilla. Pour into a greased and floured 10-inch tube pan.

Preheat oven to 375 degrees. Reduce the oven temperature to 350 degrees. Place cake in oven and bake for 15 minutes. Reduce the oven temperature to 325 degrees. Bake for 1 hour and 20 minutes or until a wooden pick inserted in the center of the cake comes out clean. Cool in the pan for 10 minutes. Remove from the pan and cool completely on a wire rack.

Combine the brown sugar, 1/4 cup milk, 2 tablespoons butter, 2 tablespoons shortening and 1 teaspoon vanilla in a saucepan. Bring to a boil. Cook for 1 minute, stirring constantly. Remove from the heat. Add enough confectioners' sugar to make of a spreading consistency. Spread the caramel icing over the cake.

Note: May serve the cake plain or with your favorite icing.

Serves Sixteen

Tucson Medical Center Auxiliary Prayer

Almighty God and Heavenly Father of Mankind, bless we pray thee, our various endeavors at Tucson Medical Center, in which we strive to bring comfort and hope to all who are in pain or distress of mind or body.

Guide us so that we may use the privilege given us to help the aged, the ill, and the very young, with generosity, with discretion, and with gentleness.

Give us the strength to labor diligently, the courage to think and to speak with clarity and conviction and without prejudice or pride.

Grant us, we beseech Thee, both wisdom and humility in directing our united efforts to do for others only as Thou would have us do.

AMEN

Mayonnaise Delight Chocolate Cake

2 cups flour, sifted
1¹/₂ cups sugar
¹/₂ cup baking cocoa
1¹/₂ teaspoons baking soda
¹/₂ teaspoon salt
1 cup warm water
³/₄ cup mayonnaise

Combine the flour, sugar, cocoa, baking soda and salt in a bowl. Add the warm water and mayonnaise and mix well. Pour into a greased 9x13-inch baking dish.

Bake at 350 degrees for 30 to 35 minutes or until a wooden pick inserted in the center comes out clean. Cool in the baking dish on a wire rack.

Spread with a fudge frosting.

Serves Sixteen

Texas Sheet Cake

1 cup margarine
1 cup water
¹/₄ cup baking cocoa
2 cups sugar
2 cups flour
¹/₂ teaspoon salt
2 eggs
¹/₂ cup sour cream
1 teaspoon baking soda
¹/₂ cup margarine
¹/₄ cup baking cocoa
¹/₄ cup plus 2 tablespoons milk
1 (1-pound) package confectioners' sugar
1 cup coarsely chopped walnuts
1 teaspoon vanilla extract

Place the 1 cup margarine, water and ¹/₄ cup cocoa in a large saucepan. Bring to a boil, stirring frequently. Remove from the heat. Add the sugar, flour and salt. Beat in the eggs, sour cream and baking soda. Pour into a greased 10x15-inch baking pan.

Bake at 375 degrees for 22 minutes or until a wooden pick inserted in the center comes out clean. Cool slightly in the pan on a wire rack.

Place the ¹/₂ cup margarine, ¹/₄ cup cocoa and milk in a saucepan. Bring to a boil, stirring frequently. Remove from the heat. Beat in the confectioners' sugar, walnuts and vanilla. Spread the frosting over the warm cake.

Serves Twelve to Sixteen

Junior Volunteers

Teenage girls began volunteering at Tucson Medical Center in 1957, working throughout the summer at various jobs. They were called Candy Stripers because of the red-and-white striped pinafores they wore. The program was very successful and, in 1963, young men were admitted to the program. They were called Junior Orderlies and worked at the main information desk.

Today, our teen Auxilians are called Junior Volunteers and are a most welcome addition to the summer staff. They can be found working in areas throughout the TMC complex. Their intelligence, abundant energy and enthusiasm, and willingness to do any job asked of them has a positive influence on patients and employees alike. It speaks well of the program when staff members who started their career at TMC as Junior Volunteers now encourage their own children to participate.

Cranberry Sauce Cake

3 cups flour
1¹/₂ cups sugar
1 cup mayonnaise
1 (16-ounce) can whole
    cranberry sauce
¹/₃ cup orange juice
1 tablespoon grated orange peel
1 teaspoon baking soda
1 teaspoon salt
1 teaspoon orange extract
1 cup chopped walnuts
1 cup confectioners' sugar
1 to 2 tablespoons orange juice

Combine the flour, sugar, mayonnaise, cranberry sauce, ¹/₃ cup orange juice, orange peel, baking soda, salt and orange extract in a bowl and mix well. Fold in the walnuts.

Cut a piece of waxed paper or parchment paper to fit the bottom of a 10-inch tube pan. Spray the pan with nonstick cooking spray and insert the paper. Spray the paper with nonstick cooking spray. Spoon the batter into the pan.

Bake at 350 degrees for 1 hour to 1 hour and 10 minutes or until a wooden pick inserted in the center of the cake comes out clean. Cool in the pan for 10 minutes. Remove from the pan to a wire rack.

Combine the confectioners' sugar and 1 tablespoon orange juice in a bowl. Drizzle the icing over the warm cake.

Serves Twelve to Sixteen

The Queen Mother's Cake

1 (8-ounce) package chopped dates
1 cup boiling water
1 teaspoon baking soda
2 1/2 cups flour
1 1/4 cups sugar
6 tablespoons butter, softened
1/2 cup chopped walnuts
1 teaspoon salt
1 teaspoon baking powder
1 teaspoon vanilla extract
1/4 cup plus 1 tablespoon packed
    brown sugar
2 tablespoons butter
2 tablespoons whipping cream or
    half-and-half

Place the dates in a large heatproof mixing bowl. Stir in the boiling water and baking soda; set aside.

Combine the flour, sugar, 6 tablespoons butter, walnuts, salt, baking powder and vanilla in a bowl. Add to the date mixture and mix well. Spoon into a greased 9x13-inch pan.

Bake at 350 degrees for 35 minutes or until a wooden pick inserted in the center comes out clean.

Combine the brown sugar, 2 tablespoons butter and whipping cream in a saucepan. Bring to a boil. Boil for 3 minutes. The consistency should be like a soft fudge. Spread the topping over the warm cake. Sprinkle additional chopped walnuts over the top of the cake if desired.

Serves Fifteen

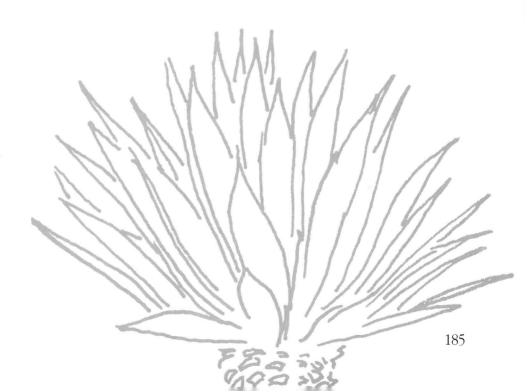

Tomato Soup Cake

2 cups sifted flour
2 teaspoons baking powder
1 teaspoon baking soda
1 teaspoon cinnamon
1 teaspoon nutmeg
1/2 teaspoon ground cloves
1/2 cup shortening
1 cup sugar
1 (10-ounce) can tomato soup
1 cup chopped pecans or walnuts
1 cup raisins
Cream Cheese Frosting

Sift the flour, baking powder, baking soda, cinnamon, nutmeg and cloves together; set aside.

Cream the shortening and sugar in a mixer bowl until light and fluffy. Add the flour mixture alternately with the tomato soup, mixing well after each addition. Stir in the pecans and raisins. Pour into a greased bundt pan.

Bake at 350 degrees for 50 to 60 minutes or until a wooden pick inserted in the center of the cake comes out clean. Cool in the pan for 10 minutes. Remove from the pan and cool completely on a wire rack. Wrap tightly in plastic wrap and let stand for 24 hours at room temperature before spreading with Cream Cheese Frosting.

Cream Cheese Frosting

3 ounces cream cheese, softened
1 1/2 cups confectioners' sugar
1 teaspoon vanilla extract

Beat the cream cheese in a mixer bowl until light and fluffy.

Add the confectioners' sugar and vanilla and beat until smooth.

Serves Ten

Piña Colada Cake

1 (2-layer) package yellow cake mix
1 (14-ounce) can sweetened condensed
  milk
1 (13-ounce) can cream of coconut
12 ounces whipped topping
1 (8-ounce) can crushed pineapple,
  drained
1 (7-ounce) can flaked coconut

Prepare the cake mix using package
directions. Pour the batter into a greased
9x13-inch pan.

Bake at 350 degrees for 30 to 35 minutes
or until a wooden pick inserted in the center
comes out clean. Poke holes in the warm
cake with a large fork.

Combine the condensed milk and cream
of coconut in a bowl. Pour over the warm
cake. Refrigerate, covered, for 8 to 10 hours.
Let stand at room temperature for 2 hours
before frosting. Combine the whipped
topping, pineapple and
coconut in a bowl. Spread the
frosting over the top of
the cake.

Serves Fifteen

TMC Security Dogs

*Who was Elmer? In reading the
history of TMC, we find that Elmer
was a lovable basset hound who
roamed the halls, escorted of course,
as the hospital mascot. Now TMC
"employs" three German shepherds
as security dogs. They are especially
trained to work with selected
members of the Tucson Medical
Center Security force.*

*It is a commentary on the times
in which we live that an institution
whose only dog was a lovable
mascot now has security dogs, who
can also be lovable, but whose main
function is to help make the TMC
campus safer for everyone.*

Tucson Medical Center Helicopter Service

In 1985, TMC was the only hospital in Arizona to have its own helicopter landing area. The Arizona Department of Public Safety proposed a four-month trial in which its helicopter and crews would be assigned at TMC. This proved to be successful and the location was made a permanent one. Emergency Room nurses were recruited and trained as flight nurses and joined the crews of the DPS Safety Air Rescue Team. This team serves all of southern Arizona, bringing in accident victims, hikers and campers located by Search and Rescue teams, and patients from outlying areas with life-threatening illnesses. The youngest of these are newborns requiring the specialized care provided in the Neonatal Intensive Care Unit.

As the helicopter service grew, a decision was made in 1989 to provide a new elevated helipad atop the Emergency Room that would accommodate several helicopters at once. New living quarters for the flight crews and office space for DPS was also included in the plan.

Special communications between the flight crew and the ER allow hospital staff to know the estimated time of arrival, condition of the patient, and treatment given en route. In turn, ER doctors can give orders for medications and monitor the patient's response. Patients are met on the helipad by medical personnel and whisked by elevator directly to the ER. The Helicopter Service is a very special part of TMC.

Turtle Cake

1 (2-layer) package German chocolate
    cake mix
1 (14-ounce) package caramels
¹/₂ cup butter
¹/₂ cup evaporated milk
1 cup chocolate chips
1 cup chopped pecans

Prepare the cake mix using package directions. Pour half the batter into a greased and floured 9x13-inch cake pan.

Bake at 350 degrees for 15 minutes.

Place the caramels, butter and evaporated milk in a saucepan. Heat over low heat until the butter and caramels are melted, stirring frequently. Pour the caramel mixture over the hot baked layer. Sprinkle with the chocolate chips and pecans. Pour the remaining cake batter over the top.

Bake for 20 minutes. Cool in the pan on a wire rack.

Note: The batter does not have to be divided exactly into halves. The cake will be fine if the caramel bubbles through the top.

Serves Fifteen

Caramels

2¹/₂ cups sugar
1 cup light corn syrup
¹/₃ cup butter
¹/₈ teaspoon cream of tartar
1³/₄ cups cream, or 1 (12-ounce) can
    evaporated milk

Combine the sugar, corn syrup, butter and cream of tartar in a heavy 2-quart saucepan. Bring to a boil, stirring constantly. Add the cream gradually, stirring constantly.

Cook over high heat to 240 to 248 degrees on a candy thermometer, firm-ball stage.

Pour into a greased 8-inch square pan. Refrigerate until cold. Cut into squares.

Serves Twenty

The Saguaro Cactus

The saguaro cactus stands like a sentinel in the Sonoran Desert, the only area in the world where it is found. Its white flower with a yellow center is the official state flower of Arizona. Attaining a height of fifty to sixty feet, and with an average life of two hundred years, it outranks all other cacti in size and longevity. Arms start to appear on the saguaro when it is about age sixty-five and as much as twelve feet tall. The trunk and arms are formed by woody ribs supporting a damp pulp. At the base of the plant, the ribs grow together to form a hub. From this hub, shallow roots extend into the desert, sponging up rainwater and distributing it through the ribs to the entire cactus. In the rainy season, the saguaro swells with the water to a weight of eighty to one hundred tons. During dry times, the cactus uses this stored water and eventually becomes thin and gaunt, with the ribs very close together.

Woodpeckers drill holes in the cactus and create a "room." To protect the plant from bleeding and dying, nature coats the walls of the "room" with a lining, forming what is known as a "saguaro boot." These boots are used by craft persons to create floral arrangements. When the woodpecker abandons the room, elf owls and other small birds take up residence.

The tips of the saguaro arms and the trunk bloom in the spring. The blossoms open for one night only and are pollinated by birds, bats, and insects. A purple seedpod develops and opens to a bright red fruit, which contains one to two thousand seeds. The fruit serves as food for the birds.

Humans eat the fruit raw or make jams and syrups from the pulp. The seeds can also be ground for flour. The Indian tribes found the saguaro fruit to be so important that the New Year began with the Month of the Saguaro Fruit Ripening. The fermented juices were used at dances held to bring the summer rains so important to agriculture.

The saguaro cactus, representing endurance, usefulness, and greatness, serves as the logo for Tucson Medical Center. At Christmas, the many saguaros on the TMC campus are decked out in red Santa Claus hats, causing all but the most Scrooge-like to smile.

Peanut Butter Fudge

1 (18-ounce) jar chunky peanut butter
1 (7-ounce) jar marshmallow creme
1 teaspoon vanilla extract
4 1/2 cups sugar
1 (12-ounce) can evaporated milk

Combine the peanut butter, marshmallow creme and vanilla in a large heatproof bowl; set aside.

Combine the sugar and evaporated milk in a saucepan. Bring to a boil over high heat, stirring constantly; reduce the heat to low. Cook for 8 minutes to 234 to 240 degrees on a candy thermometer, soft-ball stage, stirring constantly.

Pour over the peanut butter mixture and mix well. Pour onto a greased baking sheet. Cover with waxed paper and let stand at room temperature until cool.

Cut into squares and store in an airtight container.

Makes Four Pounds

Norwegian Butter Cookies

1 cup butter or margarine, softened
1 cup vegetable oil
1 cup packed brown sugar
1 cup sugar
1 egg
1 cup shredded coconut
1 cup rolled oats
1 cup crisp rice cereal
1 teaspoon salt
1 teaspoon baking soda
1 teaspoon vanilla extract
1 teaspoon cream of tartar
3 1/2 cups flour

Beat the butter, oil, brown sugar and sugar in a mixer bowl. Add the egg and mix well. Stir in the shredded coconut, oats, cereal, salt, baking soda, vanilla, cream of tartar and flour.

Refrigerate, covered, for 1 to 10 hours. Drop the dough by rounded teaspoonfuls 1 inch apart onto cookie sheets.

Bake at 350 degrees for 8 to 10 minutes or until lightly browned. Cool slightly on the cookie sheets before removing to wire racks to cool completely.

Makes Five to Seven Dozen Cookies

Double Chocolate Cookies

1 cup margarine or butter, softened
1 1/2 cups sugar
2 eggs
2 teaspoons vanilla extract
2 cups flour
2/3 cup baking cocoa
3/4 teaspoon baking soda
1/4 teaspoon salt
2 cups semisweet chocolate chips
1 cup chopped walnuts

Cream the margarine, sugar, eggs and vanilla in a large mixer bowl until light and fluffy.

Combine the flour, cocoa, baking soda and salt in a bowl. Add to the egg mixture and mix well. Stir in the chocolate chips and walnuts. Drop the dough by rounded teaspoonfuls 2 inches apart on cookie sheets.

Bake at 350 degrees for 7 to 8 minutes. Cool for 1 minute on the cookie sheets before removing the cookies to wire racks to cool completely.

Makes About Four Dozen Cookies

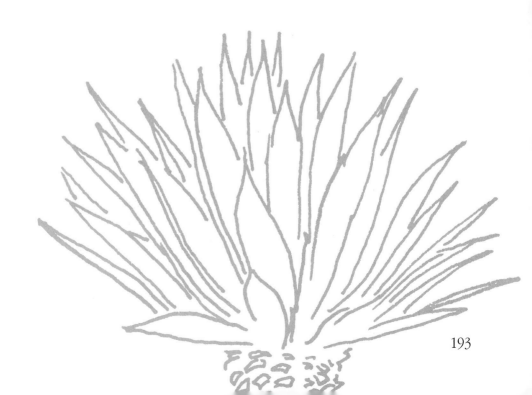

193

Make Your Own Five-Spice Powder

It's easy to make five-spice powder at home. Simply combine equal parts of cinnamon, ground cloves, ginger, and ground anise seeds. Even though this blend has only four spices, it tastes very similar to store-bought five-spice powder. Feel free to adjust the proportion of the spices to suit your tastes. Store the spice blend in an airtight jar in a cool, dry place for up to six months.

Chinese Five-Spice Oatmeal Cookies

2 cups quick-cooking oats
1¹/₂ cups flour
1 cup coarsely ground toasted almonds
1¹/₂ teaspoons five-spice powder
1 teaspoon baking powder
1 teaspoon cinnamon
¹/₂ teaspoon salt
1 cup butter or margarine, softened
1 cup sugar
1 cup packed light brown sugar
2 eggs
2 teaspoons vanilla extract

Combine the oats, flour, almonds, five-spice powder, baking powder, cinnamon and salt in a bowl; set aside.

Cream the butter, sugar and brown sugar in a large mixer bowl until light and fluffy. Add the eggs and vanilla, beating until well mixed. Beat in the flour mixture until blended. Drop the dough by rounded tablespoonfuls 1¹/₂ inches apart onto lightly greased cookie sheets.

Bake at 350 degrees for 12 to 15 minutes or until golden brown. Cool on wire racks.

Makes About Three Dozen Cookies

Cinnamon Sugar Cookies

1 cup shortening
1¹/₂ cups sugar
2 eggs
2³/₄ cups flour
2 teaspoons cream of tartar
1 teaspoon baking soda
¹/₄ teaspoon salt
2 tablespoons sugar
2 teaspoons cinnamon

Cream the shortening, 1¹/₂ cups sugar and eggs in a mixer bowl until light and fluffy.

Sift the flour, cream of tartar, baking soda and salt together. Add to the egg mixture and mix well.

Refrigerate, covered, until firm. Shape the dough into small balls.

Combine the 2 tablespoons sugar and cinnamon in a bowl. Roll the dough balls in the cinnamon-sugar mixture. Place 2 inches apart on cookie sheets.

Bake at 375 degrees for 9 to 10 minutes. Cool on wire racks.

Makes About Five Dozen Cookies

Going-to-Bed Mint Cookies

2 egg whites
$^1/_2$ teaspoon cream of tartar
$^1/_8$ teaspoon salt
$^3/_4$ cup sugar
$^1/_2$ teaspoon green or red food coloring
1 (10-ounce) package mint-flavor
   chocolate chips

Beat the egg whites, cream of tartar and salt in a large mixer bowl until foamy. Add the sugar 2 tablespoons at a time, beating constantly until the egg whites form stiff peaks.

Fold the food coloring and chocolate chips in gently. Drop the egg white mixture by teaspoonfuls onto 2 lightly greased cookie sheets.

Place the cookie sheets in a 400-degree oven. Turn off the heat immediately. Leave the cookies in the oven for 8 to 10 hours.

Makes Three Dozen Cookies

Poppy Seed Cookies

1 cup sugar
Peel of 1 orange
1 egg yolk
1 cup unsalted butter, cut into pieces
   and softened
$^1/_2$ teaspoon salt
$^1/_2$ teaspoon nutmeg
1 cup all-purpose flour
1 cup cake flour
$^1/_2$ cup poppy seeds

Place the sugar and orange peel in a food processor container. Process until the orange peel is finely chopped. Add the egg yolk. Process for 2 to 3 seconds. Add the butter, salt and nutmeg. Process for 1 minute or until light and fluffy. Add the all-purpose flour, cake flour and poppy seeds. Pulse for 4 to 5 times or just until blended. Do not overprocess.

Divide the dough into 4 equal pieces. Place each piece on a sheet of plastic wrap and shape into a 2x4-inch cylinder. Wrap the cylinders tightly in plastic wrap. Refrigerate for about 1 hour or until firm. Cut each cylinder crosswise into $^1/_4$-inch-thick slices. Place $1^1/_2$ inches apart on cookie sheets.

Bake at 350 degrees for 8 minutes or until the edges are lightly browned. Cool on wire racks.

Makes Five Dozen Cookies

Greek Butter Cookies (Kourabiedes)

1 pound whipped unsalted butter,
    softened
1 egg yolk
$1/2$ cup confectioners' sugar
2 tablespoons whiskey
5 cups flour

Beat the butter in a mixer bowl until light and fluffy. Beat in the egg yolk and confectioners' sugar. Blend in the whiskey.

Sift the flour into the butter mixture. Stir until well mixed. Shape the dough into 70 balls. Place 2 inches apart on cookie sheets.

Bake at 350 degrees for 20 to 30 minutes or until golden brown. Cool slightly on wire racks. Sprinkle the warm cookies generously with additional confectioners' sugar.

Makes Seventy Cookies

The Human Touch in Health Care

'Tis the human touch in this world
  that counts,
the touch of your hand and mine,
which means far more to the
  fainting heart
than shelter, bread, and wine.
For shelter is gone when the night is
  over,
and the bread lasts only for a day;
but the touch of the hand and the
  sound of the voice
sings in the soul always.

—Author Unknown

Raspberry Snow Bars

3/4 cup shortening
3/4 cup sugar
1/4 teaspoon salt
1/4 teaspoon almond extract
2 egg yolks
1 1/2 cups flour
1 cup raspberry preserves
1 cup flaked coconut
2 egg whites

Cream the shortening, 1/4 cup of the sugar and salt in a mixer bowl until light and fluffy. Beat in the almond extract and egg yolks. Add the flour and mix well. Pat the dough over the bottom of a 9x13-inch pan.

Bake at 350 degrees for 15 minutes. Spread the preserves over the hot crust. Top with the coconut.

Beat the egg whites in a mixer bowl until foamy. Add the remaining 1/2 cup sugar gradually, beating constantly until the egg whites form stiff peaks. Spread over the coconut.

Bake for 25 minutes. Cool in the pan on a wire rack. Cut into 24 bars.

Makes Two Dozen Bars

Oatmeal Pie

1 cup melted butter
1 cup sugar
1 cup corn syrup
1 cup rolled oats
3 eggs
1¹/₂ tablespoons brown sugar
1¹/₂ teaspoons vanilla extract
1 unbaked (9-inch) pie shell

Combine the melted butter, sugar, corn syrup, oats, eggs, brown sugar and vanilla in a bowl and mix well. Pour into the pie shell.

Bake at 350 degrees for 45 minutes or until the center is firm.

Serves Eight

Fresh Lime Pie

1 (14-ounce) can sweetened condensed
  milk
¹/₂ cup fresh lime juice
8 ounces whipped topping
2 to 3 drops of green food coloring
1 (8-inch) graham cracker crumb crust

Combine the condensed milk, lime juice, whipped topping and food coloring in a bowl and mix well. Spoon into the graham cracker crust.

Refrigerate, covered, for 2 to 3 hours.

Serves Six

Scintillating Lemon Pie

1 recipe 2-crust pie pastry
1¹/₂ tablespoons sugar
1 teaspoon nutmeg
3 lemons
1¹/₂ cups sugar
¹/₃ cup butter, softened
3 tablespoons flour
3 eggs
¹/₂ cup water

Roll half the pastry on a floured surface into a 9-inch circle. Cut into 6 wedges. Place the wedges on a baking sheet. Combine the 1¹/₂ tablespoons sugar and nutmeg in a bowl. Sprinkle over the pastry wedges.

Bake at 400 degrees for 5 minutes or until set. Remove from the baking sheet to a wire rack.

Grate the peel of the lemons. Remove and discard the white pith. Cut the lemons into very thin slices.

Cream the 1¹/₂ cups sugar, butter and flour in a mixer bowl. Beat in the eggs. Add the water and mix well. Stir in the grated peel and lemon slices.

Roll the remaining pastry on a floured surface to fit a 9-inch pie pan. Line the pie pan with the pastry. Pour the lemon mixture into the pastry shell.

Bake at 400 degrees for 25 minutes. Arrange the baked pastry wedges over the top. Bake for 5 minutes or until the filling is firm.

Serves Eight

Pineapple Pie

1 cup crushed pineapple
1 cup water
3/4 cup sugar
2 egg yolks
2 tablespoons flour
2 tablespoons cornstarch
1 tablespoon shortening
1 baked (9-inch) pie shell
2 egg whites
1/4 teaspoon salt
1/4 teaspoon vanilla extract

Place pineapple, water, 1/2 cup of the sugar, egg yolks, flour, cornstarch and shortening in a 3-quart saucepan. Cook over medium heat until bubbly and thickened, stirring constantly. Pour into the pie shell.

Beat the egg whites, salt and vanilla in a mixer bowl until the egg whites are foamy. Add the remaining 1/4 cup sugar gradually, beating constantly until stiff peaks form. Spread over the pineapple filling. Bake at 350 degrees for 12 to 15 minutes.

Serves Six to Eight

Peanut Butter Pies

4 ounces cream cheese, softened
1 cup confectioners' sugar
1/2 cup milk
1/3 cup crunchy peanut butter
12 ounces whipped topping
2 (9-inch) graham cracker crumb crusts
Chocolate syrup

Beat the cream cheese, confectioners' sugar, milk and peanut butter in a bowl until well blended. Fold in the whipped topping.

Divide the filling evenly between the graham cracker crusts. Drizzle with chocolate syrup. Freeze, covered, until ready to serve.

Serves Sixteen

201

Champion Cheesecake

1¹/₂ cups fine graham cracker crumbs
¹/₄ cup plus 2 tablespoons melted butter
¹/₄ cup sugar
16 ounces cream cheese, softened
1 cup sugar
Grated peel of 1 lemon (optional)
1 teaspoon vanilla extract
3 eggs
2 cups sour cream
3 tablespoons sugar
¹/₂ teaspoon vanilla extract

Combine the graham cracker crumbs, melted butter and ¹/₄ cup sugar in a bowl, stirring until the crumbs are evenly moistened. Press firmly over the bottom and up the side of an 8- or 9-inch springform pan. Bake at 350 degrees for 10 minutes.

Beat the cream cheese, 1 cup sugar, lemon peel and 1 teaspoon vanilla in a mixer bowl. Add the eggs and beat well. Pour into the graham cracker crust.

Bake at 350 degrees for 45 minutes. Remove from the oven. Let cool for 15 minutes. Increase the oven temperature to 475 degrees.

Combine the sour cream, 3 tablespoons sugar and ¹/₂ teaspoon vanilla in a bowl. Spread over the top of the cheesecake.

Bake for 5 minutes. Cool in the oven with the door open. Serve with fresh berries if desired.

Serves Twelve

Tucson Medical Center Auxiliary Sewing Group

Each week, a group of nimble-fingered ladies gather and sew for TMC. An early history reports that the Sewing Group hemmed forty dozen diapers. With the advent of disposable diapers, this task was eliminated. However, these ladies are not idle. Consider that in 1997 they made 522 heart shaped pillows for post-op cardiac surgery patients, 667 walker bags, 60 Easter blankets and 60 Christmas stockings for newborns, 138 splints, plus 250 other items as requested by various departments in the hospital. Way to go, ladies! Keep those sewing machines humming, scissors snipping, and needles threaded. The hospital needs you and the patients love your efforts.

Cranberry Mincemeat Ice Cream

1 quart fresh or frozen cranberries
1/2 gallon vanilla ice cream
1 (28-ounce) jar mincemeat with brandy and rum
1/2 cup chopped pecans or walnuts

Place the cranberries in a large microwave-safe dish. Microwave, loosely covered, on High until the cranberries pop, stirring once. Cool completely. Soften the ice cream, reserving the carton. Add the mincemeat to the cooled cranberries and mix well.

Spoon the softened ice cream into a bowl. Stir in half the cranberry mixture and the pecans. Return the ice cream mixture to the carton. Freeze until firm. Refrigerate the remaining cranberry mixture for later use.

Serves Ten

Tucson Medical Center Emergency Room

The Emergency Room is one of the busiest areas of any hospital and one of the most important assets of the hospital to the community. The Emergency Room at Tucson Medical Center opened in 1945 in one twelve by fourteen-foot room serving about one hundred patients a month. Most of these were skiers or hikers injured on Mount Lemmon or in Sabino Canyon.

To meet community demand, the Emergency Room was expanded in 1953 and again in 1959. A new Emergency Room was constructed as part of the outpatient area remodel in 1980. Twenty-two beds were available to handle some twenty-five hundred patients a month. The TMC Auxiliary gave $100,000 to help furnish this

ultramodern facility. Paramedics were added to the ER staff in 1984.

As Tucson grew, so did the need for yet more ER space and state-of-the-art equipment. TMC Auxiliary pledged $500,000 for this project. This new area opened in 1995 and is rated a Level One Trauma Unit. Caring for fifty thousand patients a year, the staff is highly trained and very efficient.

In 1998, a Courtesy Desk, shared with the Urgent Care area, was established, staffed by Auxilians and employees. Greeting new arrivals, the volunteers act as a liaison between the family and friends in the waiting area and the patient in the treatment area. If appropriate, they also spend some time with the patient, attempting to make their stay as positive as possible.

Strawberry Dessert

6 ounces vanilla wafers
1/2 cup butter, softened
2 cups confectioners' sugar
2 eggs
2 cups crushed strawberries
1 cup ground nuts
1 cup whipping cream
Vanilla extract to taste
Confectioners' sugar to taste

Place the vanilla wafers in a plastic food storage bag. Crush with a rolling pin to form crumbs. Sprinkle half the crumbs over the bottom of a 9x13-inch baking dish.

Combine the butter, 2 cups confectioners' sugar and eggs in a bowl and mix well. Spread over the crumbs in the dish.

Combine the strawberries and nuts in a bowl. Spread over the butter mixture.

Whip the whipping cream with vanilla and confectioners' sugar to taste. Spread over the strawberries.

Refrigerate, covered, for at least 4 hours. Cut into squares to serve.

Serves Twelve

Cream Puffs

1 cup water
¹⁄₄ cup shortening
¹⁄₈ teaspoon salt
1 cup sifted flour
4 eggs
Vanilla pudding or ice cream
Chocolate icing or chocolate sauce
Whipped cream

Bring the water to a boil in a large saucepan. Add the shortening and salt. Return to a boil; reduce the heat to low. Add the flour and stir vigorously until the mixture forms a ball that leaves the side of the pan. Remove from the heat.

Add the eggs 1 at a time, beating well after each addition. Beat until the dough is thick, shiny and smooth. Drop the dough by teaspoonfuls or tablespoonfuls onto baking sheets.

Bake at 450 degrees for 20 minutes. Reduce the oven temperature to 350 degrees. Bake for 20 minutes or until golden brown. Let cool on wire racks.

Make a slit in the side of each puff and fill with pudding. Spread chocolate icing over the tops. May remove the tops from the puffs and fill with ice cream, replacing the tops and serving with chocolate sauce and whipped cream.

Makes One Dozen Large or Four Dozen Small Cream Puffs

Jellied Irish Coffee

1/2 cup cold water
1 envelope unflavored gelatin
1 1/2 cups hot water
1/4 cup sugar
1/4 cup Irish whiskey
1 1/2 teaspoons instant coffee granules
Whipped cream

Pour the cold water into a medium saucepan. Sprinkle the gelatin over the water and let stand until softened. Add the hot water. Heat for 2 to 3 minutes or until the gelatin is dissolved, stirring constantly.

Add the sugar, whiskey and instant coffee and stir to blend. Pour into a bowl. Refrigerate, covered, until set. Serve with whipped cream.

Note: May cut the jellied coffee into cubes and serve in coffee cups with small cookies.

Serves Six

Celebration Fruit Punch

2 (64-ounce) bottles grape juice
4 cups lemonade
2 cups orange juice
2 cups apple juice
1 package frozen pineapple chunks

Combine the grape juice, lemonade, orange juice, apple juice and pineapple in a punch bowl. Serve over ice.

Serves Forty-Eight

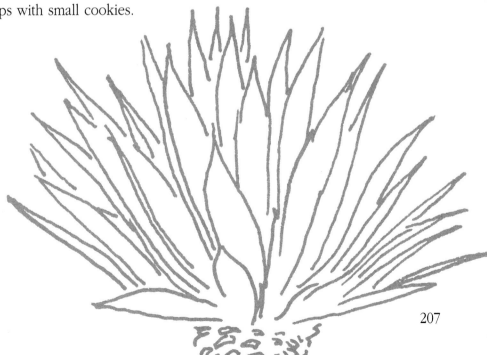

Mexican Fruit Punch

3 cups chopped papaya (1¹/₂ pounds)
3 cups chopped fresh pineapple
    (1¹/₂ pounds)
3 cups fresh orange juice
1 cup chopped watermelon (8 ounces)
4 cups water
¹/₃ cup sugar

Place the papaya, pineapple, orange juice and watermelon in a blender container. Process until puréed. Pour into a pitcher. Stir in the water and sugar.

Serve over ice, garnished with small pineapple chunks.

Serves Six to Eight

Champagne Punch

1 cup water
¹/₂ cup sugar
1 cup grapefruit juice
¹/₂ cup orange juice
¹/₄ cup grenadine syrup
1 (750-milliliter) bottle pink Champagne,
    chilled

Combine the water and sugar in a saucepan. Bring to a boil; reduce the heat to low. Simmer, uncovered, just until the sugar is dissolved, stirring constantly. Cool to room temperature.

Combine the sugar syrup, grapefruit juice, orange juice and grenadine syrup in a pitcher. Refrigerate until chilled.

When ready to serve, pour the juice mixture into a punch bowl. Add the Champagne. Serve over ice, garnished with twists of lemon peel and maraschino cherries with stems.

Serves Ten to Twelve

Sangría

4 cups dry red wine
4 cups mineral water
³/₄ cup grenadine syrup
³/₄ cup fresh lime juice
1 orange, thinly sliced
¹/₂ cup chopped peeled peach or
*   pineapple*

Combine the wine, mineral water, grenadine syrup and lime juice in a glass pitcher and mix well. Stir in the orange slices and peach.
    Refrigerate until chilled. Add ice cubes just before serving.

Serves Six to Eight

Bob Wheeler's Margaritas

2 to 3 small ice cubes
9 ounces margarita mix
3 ounces tequila
⁷/₈ ounce Triple Sec

Place the ice cubes, margarita mix, tequila and Triple Sec in a blender container. Process until well blended.
    Pour into salt-rimmed margarita glasses.

Serves Three

Tucson Medical Center
Bob Wheeler,
Food Service Director 1969–1985

Tucson Medical Center Auxiliary Remembrance Fund

The Remembrance Fund was established by the Auxiliary as a fund-raiser and a venue for individuals to honor the memory of family members and friends or to commemorate a special occasion or happening. The monies received are incorporated into the annual gift to Tucson Medical Center from the Auxiliary. Donors are recognized in the TMC Foundation publication "ON CENTER." The Remembrance Fund is a special part of the Auxiliary and receives many generous donations.

Bourbon Slush

1 (6-ounce) can lemonade concentrate
1 (6-ounce) can orange juice concentrate
1 cup sugar
1 cup strong brewed tea (6 tea bags)
7 cups water
2 cups bourbon
Lemon-lime soda or ginger ale

Combine the lemonade and orange juice concentrates in a gallon container. Add the sugar to the brewed tea. Stir until the sugar is completely dissolved. Add the tea to the concentrates. Stir in the water and bourbon, mixing well. Freeze for at least 24 hours to form a slush.

To serve, fill each glass halfway with the bourbon slush. Pour in enough soda to fill the glass and stir. Serve with a straw and garnish with a maraschino cherry and fresh mint sprig.

Makes One Gallon Slush

Kahlúa Tumbleweed

7 cups sugar
6 cups water
3 ounces instant coffee granules
1 quart 196 proof grain alcohol
1/4 cup plus 2 tablespoons vanilla extract

Combine the sugar and 5 cups of the water in a saucepan. Bring to a boil. Boil for 5 minutes. Remove from the heat; set aside.

Combine the remaining 1 cup water and instant coffee in another saucepan. Bring to a boil. Remove from the heat. Add the coffee mixture to the sugar syrup and mix well.

Cool to room temperature. Stir in the grain alcohol and vanilla.

Makes About Ten Cups

Sherry Eggnog

4 egg yolks
1 cup sugar
2 quarts milk
1 bottle cream sherry
4 egg whites
Freshly grated or ground nutmeg

Beat the egg yolks in a large mixer bowl until thick and creamy. Add 3/4 cup of the sugar gradually, beating until the sugar is dissolved. Stir in the milk and sherry.

Refrigerate, covered, until chilled. Beat the egg whites in a mixer bowl until stiff peaks form. Beat in the remaining 1/4 cup sugar gradually. Spoon the beaten egg whites into a punch bowl. Pour in the sherry mixture and blend. Sprinkle nutmeg over the top.

Serves Twenty-Four

TMC Holiday Eggnog

9 egg yolks
1/4 teaspoon salt
1/3 cup sugar
3/4 cup Myers' rum
3/4 cup Bacardi light rum
9 egg whites, at room temperature
3 cups milk
1 quart light cream

Beat the egg yolks and salt in a large mixer bowl until the egg yolks are thickened and pale yellow. Add the sugar gradually, beating constantly. Add the dark and light rums gradually, beating well.

Beat the egg whites in a mixer bowl until stiff peaks form. Stir into the egg yolk mixture. Stir in the milk and cream gradually, blending well.

Refrigerate, covered, for 2 to 3 hours or until well chilled. Serve in punch cups, sprinkled with freshly ground nutmeg.

Serves Twenty-Four

Tucson Medical Center
Bob Wheeler,
Food Service Director 1969–1985

Hot Spiced Wassail

2 (6-inch) sticks cinnamon
1 tablespoon whole allspice
16 whole cloves
3 small oranges
6 cups apple juice
2 cups cranberry juice
1/4 cup sugar
1 cup rum (optional)

Break the cinnamon sticks into pieces. Place in a cheesecloth bag with the allspice. Insert the cloves in the oranges.

Combine the apple juice, cranberry juice and sugar in a large saucepan. Add the oranges and spice bag.

Bring to a boil. Simmer, covered, for 15 minutes. Add the rum and heat through.

Remove the spice bag and oranges before serving.

Serves Eight to Ten

The TMC Chapel

By Jane Schotland, Auxilian 1986

Tones of earth, tones of sky,
Reaching out to all in pain,
Offering that inner peace,
Sunlight after clouds and rain.

Letting faith renew the soul,
Blessing with the strength to cope,
Pushing back the black despair,
Turning on the light of hope.

Binding up the wounds of grief,
Soothing every troubled heart,
Colors from a universe
In which each plays an equal part.

Tones of earth, tones of sky,
Helping banish doubt and fear,
Affirmation of the creed:
We treat more than illness here.

213

CONTRIBUTORS

Our cookbook committee would like to express their appreciation for the wonderful response of our contributors. However, because of the limitation of space, we were unable to include every recipe. Our thanks to each of you for sharing the "treasures" from your kitchen.

Lou Bankson
Joan Berry
Sara Block
Sue Blye
Marty Bortle
Katie Brooks
E.J. Burson
Carolyn W. Carter
Joyce Christianson
Susan Christie
Diane Clover
Dorothy Collins
Arlene Crawford
Eva Damschroder
Bobbie Danneberg
Kitty Davis
Rose Davis
Joseph C. DeAcetis
Mary C. DeAcetis
Lillian Deo
Percy Diamontopoulos
Ursicina Dos Santos
Donna Durns
Norma Fletcher
Edna Foster

Bill Foster
Marilyn Fulton
Andrea Gabbert
Lucy Gilbert
Shirley Gould
Dorothy Grant
Gail Greeley
Mrs. William S. Gregg
Gyn. Women's Surgery
Hila Hansen
Rose Hanson
Rose Marie Hartsky
Betty Hawkins
Marjorie Heath
Heidi Herrington
Elsie Hill
Marilyn Hulkower
Helen Ivory
Trudy Jaskela
Ivette Jimenez-Ott
Jean Kearns
Ellen M. Kightlinger
JoAnn Kilpatrick
Pat Knoblock
Naomi Komacek

Bonnie Kostka
Rebecca Kowren
Catherine LaFave
Barbara Lawrie
David Lilley
George MacMonagle
Barbara Marks
Sue Mason
Carolyn Matson
Yevonda May
Eunice Milliron
Catherine Morris
Kathy Nardozza
Marcia Notheis
Lois Peck
Veda Petrie
Nycee Randall
Gen Raymer
Pat Reinhart
Helen Reynolds
Toni Rockfeld
Marian Rogerson
Fama K. Rounds
Frances F. Rubiner
Wanda R. Russell

Cameron Sandhowe
Florence L. Saltzman
Marge Schmidt
Mary Ruth Shropshire
Margaret Shunk
Phyllis Simansky
Helen Smith
Mathilde Snell
Harriet Spiesman
Millie M. Spillane
Melissa Stevens
Marian Tapas
Kate Thiem
Muriel Thomasson
Michele Tinsley
Ibby Ulmer
Ed Van Metre
Jerie Vaughn
Rosemarie Volz
Kelly Wallace-Howell
Eleanore Wickham
Barbara Winter
Cleo Wipff

Chefs and Restaurants

Bob Wheeler, Food Service Director, TMC
Tucson Medical Center
Todd Seligman, Executive Chef, TMC
Scott Schupmann, Chef, TMC
Jonathan Landeen, Owner-Chef, Jonathan's Tucson Cork
Stephan Michallet-Ferrier, Executive Chef, Anthony's in
    the Catalinas
Joeseph Dessault, Executive Chef, Charles Restaurant
Kay Roberts, Chef, Ye Olde Lantern
Alan Sanchez, Executive Chef, Tack Room
Issa Moussa, Executive Chef, Skyline Country Club
Donna Nordin, Owner-Chef, Café Terra Cotta
Mark A. Shelton, Executive Chef, Tanque Verde Guest Ranch
Buddy's Grill
Tom Gerlak, Executive Chef, Doubletree Hotel

215

REFLECTIONS INDEX

RECIPE INDEX

TUCSON TREASURES
Recipes & Reflections

Tucson Medical Center Auxiliary
5301 East Grant Road
Tucson, Arizona 85712
(520) 324-5359 or (800) 526-5353 ext. 45359
Website: www.tmcaz.com

Please send _____ copies of **TUCSON TREASURES Recipes & Reflections** at $21.95 each $ _____

Postage and handling at $3.05 each $ _____

Total $ _____

_____
Name

_____
Street Address

_____
City   State   Zip

(_____)
Daytime Telephone

Method of Payment: [   ] VISA   [   ] MasterCard
                      [   ] Check enclosed payable to TMC Auxiliary

_____
Account Number   Expiration Date

_____
Cardholder Name

_____
Signature

Photocopies accepted.